Arise
Fly High
Float Free

WestBow Press books may be ordered through booksellers or by contacting:

WestBow Press
A Division of Thomas Nelson & Zondervan
1663 Liberty Drive
Bloomington, IN 47403
www.westbowpress.com
1 (866) 928-1240

Because of the dynamic nature of the Internet, any web addresses or links contained in this book may have changed since publication and may no longer be valid. The views expressed in this work are solely those of the author and do not necessarily reflect the views of the publisher, and the publisher hereby disclaims any responsibility for them.

Any people depicted in stock imagery provided by Getty Images are models, and such images are being used for illustrative purposes only. Certain stock imagery © Getty Images.

ISBN: 978-1-9736-8930-0 (sc)
ISBN: 978-1-9736-8931-7 (e)

Library of Congress Control Number: 2020906926

Print information available on the last page.

WestBow Press rev. date: 01/18/2021

WESTBOW
PRESS®
A DIVISION OF THOMAS NELSON
& ZONDERVAN

This book is dedicated to my wife and best friend for 48 years, Lois Christine Bailey Wojcik, who lost her fight with cancer on Christmas Eve, 2011. She inspired me throughout our life together to live my dreams and become more than I ever thought I could be. In honor of her memory, all proceeds for this book will go to St. Jude's Children's Research Hospital in hopes of helping others to be able to live their dreams as well.

Lois Christine Bailey Wojcik

July 26, 1947 - December 24, 2011

Contents

Introduction

"For I am not ashamed of the gospel of Christ for it is the power of God unto salvation to everyone that believeth, to the Jew first, and also to the Greek. For therein is the righteousness of God revealed from faith to faith: as it is written the just shall live by faith. For the wrath of God is revealed from heaven against all ungodliness and unrighteousness of men who hold the truth In unrighteousness: Because that which may be known of God is manifest in them: for God hast showed [it] unto them. For the invisible things of him from the creation of the world are clearly seen. being understood by the things that are made, [even] his eternal power and Godhead so that they are without excuse." Romans 1:16-20

In the 70's, a popular television series, "Kung Fu," featured a young disciple of a Chinese religious philosophy. His teacher was a blind man who would constantly point out various things that the young disciple, though he had eyes failed to see. In one episode the young boy asked his teacher "Old man, how is it that you see all these things?" The blind man replied "How is it that you do not?"

This dramatic lesson illustrates a truth that is tragically evident in today's world. Millions of people are blind to the presence of God around them. The bible tells us that *"the invisible things of him* [God] *from the creation of the world are clearly seen."* The presence of God and his handiwork is demonstrated in every aspect of Life. No matter where you look, there are illustrations of how God works in the life of a man or woman. All we need do is look to see them.

Certainly, the art of preaching demonstrates this fact. A good preacher can take an everyday occurrence and effectively communicate gospel truths in his sermons. This fact illustrates Paul's statement that *"..the invisible things of him [God] are clearly seen..."*

I hope that the following illustrations will entertainingly communicate some gospel truths and allow you, the reader, to see God and the Christian experience in a way that you may have never considered. May it also serve to open your eyes to the world around you and *"the things of God that are clearly seen"* within it.

Arise, Fly High and Float Free

For as long as I can remember I've been fascinated with airplanes and the realm of flight. The thought that through them I could achieve the age-old desire of mankind to "break free of the pull of the earth's gravitational force and soar freely through the sky" inspired me to achieve my private pilot license while still a teenager and my commercial license at the age of twenty.

For years now I had enjoyed an occasional escape from the earth's gravitational boundaries. However, it wasn't until the spring of 1991 that I discovered the true freedom I sought in "lighter-than-air" flight in a hot air balloon. Now, having spent thousands of hours aloft in both powered and lighter-than-air aircraft, I have come to see several interesting similarities between lighter-than-air flight and another age-old quest of man: the desire to be free from the controlling force which sin has on us and the desire to float freely in the grace of God. This book explores those similarities while attempting to illustrate the concepts of...

"Arising"
above our sinful nature,
don't you know that as many of us as were baptized into Christ Jesus were baptized into His death? Therefore we were buried with Him through baptism into death, that just as Christ was raised from the dead by the glory of the Father, even so we also sh ould walk in newness of life.
Rom 6:3-4

"Flying High"
above the controlling force that sin has on us,
Even the youths shall faint and be weary, And the young men shall utterly fall, But those who wait on the LORD Shall renew their strength; They shall mount up with wings like eagles,
Isa 40:30-31

and

"Floating Free"
in God's unmerited Grace. But now we are set free from the power of sin and belong to God,
and his benefits to us include holiness and everlasting life.
For the wages of sin is death, but the free gift of God is eternal life through Jesus Christ our Lord. Romans 6:22-23

1] The Two Vehicles of Flight

Over the past hundred years man has devised many different type of vehicles that have allowed him to break free of the earth's gravitational force. However, all of them can be placed into two general categories: powered and lighter-than-air.

Powered:

All powered aircraft have some major similarities. They include the "power source" that propels it and components like the wings, ailerons, elevators and vertical stabilizer which allow the pilot directional and altitude control. Even gliders require a power source to gain altitude, then they have complete directional control to work air currents to remain aloft.

Lighter-than-air:

Lighter-than-air vehicles simply have a source of lift, either gas or hot air. The hot air balloon has the additional component of a burner to heat the air that keeps it aloft. While technically the burner is a source of power, it is not the burner that keeps the balloon aloft but the power of the heated air within it that allows it to overcome the gravitational force which holds all things in its power. However, neither the hot air nor the gas balloon has a source of directional control other then the natural elements in which it floats…the air itself. As the direction in which the air travels commonly changes with altitude, the direction in which the balloon travels can be changed by changing altitude. This is accomplished by heating the air within the balloon. Also, generally speaking, as altitude increases, the speed of the air usually also increases. So as the balloon gains altitude, it can travel faster and thus further.

Religion:

Throughout history man has continually tried to devised ways to worship some deity which he recognizes as being the source of his benefits and protection. We commonly refer to these various ways as "religion." However, despite their many diversities, all religions can be placed into two categories: man-powered and God-powered.

Man-powered:

All man-powered religions have major similarities. They include a supreme being who inspires man to be more than he is, and rules, traditions and ceremonies that man performs to lift him above his nature and make him acceptable to that supreme being. Just as in powered flight where a pilot is in control of his direction of travel and ultimate destination, "man-powered" religion gives man the power to control his destiny by his decisions and actions.

God-powered:

God-powered "religion" simply has a "power source" that "lifts" man above his sinful nature, frees him from the "pull" of sin and makes him acceptable to God. That power source is God himself. As in "lighter-than-air" flight where air fills a balloon and the balloon becomes part of the air surrounding it, the Spirit of God fills a man and he becomes part of that Spirit, the body of Christ which we refer to as the "church."

Just as hot air fills a balloon and empowers it to become what it was created to be, God fills a man and empowers him to be what he was created to be. Just as the heated air within the balloon allows it to break free from the pull of gravity which holds it down, the Spirit of God is the power source which fills a man and allows him to break free from the pull of sin, ascend above life's sinful influences and float free from those influences.

A balloon becomes part of the column of air in which it enters as it ascends away from the pull of the earth. It then travels in the same direction and speed along with the column of air it enters. A person filled by the Spirit of God also becomes part of that Spirit which becomes the directing force of that person's life, taking them to their ultimate destination.

A hot-air-balloon pilot can only control how hot the air is within the balloon, thus, how high the balloon ultimately raises. As previously mentioned, generally speaking, the higher a balloon flies, the faster and farther it goes as wind speed tends to increase with altitude. A person can also control how "hot" the Spirit of God is within them through their relationship with God as they pray, study and meditate on God's Word. The "hotter" they are, the "higher" they fly [so to speak], the faster they mature and the further they progress in their Christian walk. Therefore, the more they can accomplish for God as His Spirit works within them.

In which type of the above two vehicles [religion] are you traveling through life to your ultimate destination? Are you trying to control your destiny through "works," or are you relying on God's Spirit for grace and directional guidance?

2] Form and Function

The Balloon:

Although they come in many different colors, shapes, and sizes, balloons are easily discernible apart from any of God's or man's other creations which occupy the realm that surrounds our planet. A balloon is constructed of nylon, the same material used to produce other everyday household objects. Nylon is a tough but light-weight fabric which, when stitched together in a particular form, can perform the function for which a balloon is designed, …flight.

Balloons come in various sizes ranging from a little over thirty thousand, to well over two hundred thousand cubic feet in volume. As form determines function, size determines purpose. Smaller balloons are more maneuverable, while larger balloons carry more weight. Balloons can also come in various colors and shapes, some taking on the appearance of some well-known object or character. Despite their color, size, or shape, balloons all have one thing in common, a large chamber filled with air, which, when heated, overcomes the effects of gravity on the aircraft.

When a balloon is taken out of its carrying bag and laid out on the ground, it does not resemble what it is, but appears to be nothing more than a pile of colorful cloth. As a large gas-powered fan fills the balloon with air, it begins to take on the characteristic form of what it is. However, the balloon cannot perform the function for which it was designed until the air inside of it is heated.

Man:

Of all God's creations, man is unique. Although we come in many different colors, shapes, and sizes, and are constructed out of the same basic materials that every other living object that occupies this planet is made of, we are uniquely different. As with any other object, form determines function. Of all of his creations, God created man for a particular function - to fill us with His Holy Spirit so we can "let our light so shine before men that they might see our good works and glorify God" [Matthew 5:16].

When a man is first created he does not resemble what he will ultimately become, he simply resembles a mass of cells. When God breathes into him the "breath of life," [Genesis 2:7] those cells begin to take on the characteristic form of what they will become, a person. However, until God "heats" the life within him through the presence of the Holy Spirit [John 3:3, 1 John 5:11–12, Romans 8:9], man cannot complete the task for which he was created [Ephesians 2:10], to love and serve God as ministers of reconciliation to a lost and dying world [2 Corithians 5:17–18].

3] Laws...

Man-made and Natural Laws:

There are man-made laws, and there are natural laws. While man-made laws are easily broken, natural laws are not. An example of natural law is the law of gravity. This law is illustrated by holding something in your hand then releasing it. No matter where you are on this planet or in this universe, the law of gravity applies. We are all governed by this law and it cannot be broken. However, it can be overcome by another, but a higher law of nature.

When a parcel of air is heated, it becomes lighter than the air around it and it rises to overcome the law of gravity. If that parcel of air is contained into a confined space and a vehicle is attached to it, that vehicle will rise with the heated air. Thus, anyone within that vehicle can also overcome the law of gravity. That is the principle of lighter-than-air flight in a hot air balloon.

Spiritual Laws:

There is a third type of law which governs man, spiritual law. One of those laws is the law of sin. It is illustrated in the seventh chapter of the book of Romans. In that chapter Paul observes that whenever he tried to do what is right and good, he ended up doing the opposite. He concluded the following:

"For I delight in the law of God according to the inward man. But I see another law in my members, warring against the law of my mind and bringing me into captivity to the **law of sin** which is in my members. O wretched man that I am! Who will deliver me from this body of death?" Romans 7: 22-24 [NKJV]

Just as man is subject to the law of gravity, he is also subject to the law of sin. Every person who has ever lived is a sinner [Romans 3:23] and God's Word [The Bible] tells us that the consequences of that sin is death. [Romans 6:23] Like gravity, the law of sin cannot be broken. However, like gravity, the law of sin can be overcome by a higher law, ...the law of Grace.

"Therefore, there is now no condemnation for those who are in Christ Jesus, because through Christ Jesus the law of the Spirit of life set me free from the law of sin and death." Romans 8:12

The law of Grace states that God's love is greater than sin. Just as the heated air which fills a balloon allows it to overcome the law of gravity, God's Spirit can fill a person and enable them to overcome the law of sin.

"But we have been set free from the power of sin and belong to God, and his benefit to us is holiness and eternal life." Romans 6:22

4] The Power Within

The average balloon comes in a canvas bag that is little more than three or four feet in diameter and four feet high. It is difficult for a newcomer to the sport to appreciate that this rather small package contains an object that will eventually stand nearly eighty feet tall and extend nearly seventy feet at its widest point. The balloon attaches to a basket containing the fuel tanks, the burner which heats the air, the flight instruments, pilot, and passengers. When fully assembled, the aircraft can weigh from several hundred to over a thousand pounds.

The power to lift this amount of weight comes from the unseen heated air inside of the balloon. The energy that heats that air comes from a fuel source, propane. Propane is used because it has a low boiling point of -44F. Although propane is a liquid, by the time its temperature is raised to what we consider freezing [32F], it is in a gaseous state. That gas is converted into usable energy by the burner which ignites the gas, producing heat.

The burner is a remarkable instrument capable of converting a rather small amount of propane gas into an enormous amount of energy. The burner output is rated in BTUs [British Thermal Units]. A BTU is the amount of energy that it takes to raise one pound of water one degree Fahrenheit. Some manufacturers claim their burners can produce as much power as 12 to 24 <u>million</u> BTUs in an hour.

In the book of 1 Samuel, the Bible gives an account of a boy named David, who confronted a giant of a man named Goliath. Although his adversary was considerably larger, stronger, and well-armed, David was able to defeat this enemy by the power of God that existed within him. That power came in the form of God's Holy Spirit, which was converted into spiritual strength by the instrument of faith.

Those who witnessed David's encounter with Goliath found it difficult to appreciate that this small lad contained the power to raise to enormous proportions and accomplish a feat beyond his apparent capacity. The Bible tells us that this same power is available to us. When it is converted into spiritual energy through faith, we can "move mountains," "conquer spiritual wickedness," and do "more than we ask or can imagine." The power of God within us "renews our strength." It enables us to "run and not grow weary" and allows us to "mount up with wings as eagles," soaring above sin and floating in a peace which "passes all understanding."

David, like a balloon, illustrates that fact that you cannot judge the capacity of an object [or person] by its size when it is driven by an unseen power within.

"God gives power to the weak, and to those who have no might He increases their strength. Even the youths shall grow faint and be weary, and the young men shall utterly fall, but those who wait on the LORD shall renew their strength; they shall mount up with wings like eagles, they shall run and not be weary, they shall walk and not faint." Isaiah 40:29-31

Arise Fly High Float Free • 9

5] Floating Vs. Flying

Unlike an airplane that travels through the air, a balloon hangs suspended in a column of air. As that column moves across the sky, the balloon moves with it. Therefore, the balloon more resembles a cloud than a plane, and it is more correct to say that it "floats" than to say that it "flies," ...although ballooning is commonly referred to as "flying" and not floating. Flying implies work and suggests some action is performed to suspend the vehicle in the air. Floating implies rest and ease.

Generally speaking, air covers the earth in layers. Each layer can travel at a different speed and in a different direction. Therefore, as a balloon ascends into different layers of air, those layers can change the direction and speed of the balloon's flight. However, the balloon and the column of air it rides in remain as one, traveling at the same speed and in the same direction.

As the balloon travels through the sky it is held aloft by the air <u>inside</u> of it, but is propelled and directed by the air <u>surrounding</u> it. It is the air that makes the balloon what it is. It gives the balloon its form and function; it suspends it above the earth free of the pull of gravity and directs it along its path. In a very real way, the balloon is as much a part of the air as the air is a part of the balloon.

A person is a Christian because he has the Spirit of God living within him [Rom 8:9-11, 1 John 5:11-12] and because he lives within that Spirit himself. As the air fills a balloon giving it its form and allowing it to perform the function for which it was created, the Spirit of God fills a man, making him a new creature and empowering him to perform the task for which he was created. As the air within the balloon enables it to rise and overcome the pull of gravity, it is the Spirit of God in man that enables him to rise above his sinful nature and overcome the pull of sin. As the air directs and propels the balloon along its course of travel, it is the Spirit of God that guides and leads a man through life.

"Those who live according to a sinful nature have their minds set on what that nature desires, and those who live by the Spirit of God have their minds set on what God's Spirit desires. The mind of a sinful man leads him to death, but the mind controlled by the Spirit of God leads to life and peace. The sinful mind is hostile to God. It does not submit to God's law, nor can it do so. Therefore, those controlled by that sinful nature cannot please God. However, one is not controlled by that sinful nature, but by the Spirit of God, if that Spirit lives within them. <u>If a man does not have the Spirit of Christ within him, he does not belong to Christ</u>. But if Christ is <u>in</u> him, his body is dead because of sin, but his spirit is alive because of righteousness. And if the Spirit of him who raised Jesus from the dead is living in you, he who raised Christ from the dead will also give life to your mortal bodies through his Spirit, who lives in you." Romans 8:5-11

6] A Peaceful Flight

Of all the differences that exist between flying in an airplane and flying in a hot air balloon, the most remarkable is the smoothness and peacefulness of the experience. Anyone who has ever flown in an airplane knows that it can be loud and very bumpy. That is because an airplane can have a powerful and loud engine, and is continuously passing through different columns of air as it moves through the sky.

As the earth is heated by the sun, it, in turn heats the air around it. However, the earth is heated unevenly; thus it heats the air directly in contact with it unevenly. Sandy ground and developed areas tend to reflect the sun's energy, warming the air over it rapidly. Water and wooded areas tend to absorb the sun's energy, heating the air over it slowly. Therefore, air tends to rise in uneven columns of energy as it is heated over the different areas that make up our planet. As an airplane passes through these columns, it experiences lift in columns of greater energy, and it loses lift in columns of lesser energy, raising and dropping like a car driving over a very bumpy road.

A balloon rides in a single column of air as it passes over the ground. It travels in the same direction and at the same speed as that column. Thus, it does not encounter any of the bumpiness that is associated with the powered flight of an airplane as that vehicle passes from one column of air to another column of air. To know what lighter-than-air flight is like, one must only close their eyes and stand quietly. There is no feeling of movement; thus there can be no airsickness. Except for the occasional blast of the burner to maintain the temperature of the constantly cooling air within the balloon, there is no sound other than that of the natural things that it passes over.

Life can be rather noisy and full of distractions as we pass through the ups and downs of a typical day, resulting in mental and physical stress. However, the Bible tells us that we need not worry about anything if we maintain a close personal relationship with Christ [Phil 4:4-9]. We can do that by beginning our day with God, then walk closely with God throughout our day by prayer and meditation of his Word which we hide in our hearts, and by focusing on things that are...

"...true and good and right. Think about things that are pure and lovely, and dwell on the fine, good things in others. Think about all you can praise God for and be glad about. Keep putting into practice all you learned from me and saw me doing, and the God of peace will be with you." Phil 4:8-9 [The Living Bible]

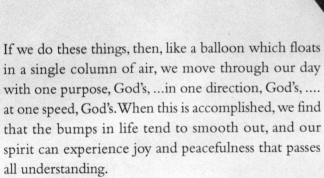

If we do these things, then, like a balloon which floats in a single column of air, we move through our day with one purpose, God's, ...in one direction, God's, ... at one speed, God's. When this is accomplished, we find that the bumps in life tend to smooth out, and our spirit can experience joy and peacefulness that passes all understanding.

7] Staying Hot

Nylon is the most commonly used material in the construction of a balloon. It is very strong, yet it is very light in weight. While it will puncture, it will not tear easily. Another reason it is preferred, it does not burn! Nylon melts at approximately 450F. Therefore, if the flame of the burner directly contacts the fabric it may melt a hole in it but the fabric will not ignite.

For all its strengths, nylon has one major weakness; it is a poor insulator and loses heat rapidly. The air inside of the balloon must be kept at a temperature sufficient to maintain lift and overcome the pull of gravity. Therefore, heat has to be replaced with frequent consistency. Throughout the flight, the burner must be turned on [or blasted] for several seconds every minute and sometimes several times a minute. As soon as the burner is turned off the air in the balloon begins to cool. As lift is lost, the pull of gravity becomes stronger and stronger until the balloon begins to rapidly descend.

Like a balloon, man is a poor insulator of God's Spirit and tends to "cool" rapidly. To stay "hot," man must stay in constant touch with God through reading his Word [the Bible], prayer and meditation on God's Word. If man is separated from God, his spirit [not God's] will begin to "cool" and the pull of sin will become stronger and stronger until man begins a rapid descent into the sinful influences that God saved him from. Therefore, God must intercede. This principle is beautifully illustrated in God's Word:

"For by one offering he hath perfected forever them that are sanctified." Hebrews 10:14

God sent his Son Jesus Christ to die for our sins. Christ's death was the "offering," or "sacrifice" that had to be paid for our sinfulness. By that sacrifice, God "perfected" us. The Word perfected in the original Greek language is "teleioo," which means to complete or finish. God's Word tells us that God did this "forever." The word "forever" in the original Greek language is "dienekes," and means "perpetually" or "continually."

Just as the air in a balloon keeps it aloft and free from the influences of gravity by **"<u>continually</u>"** heating it, God's Spirit keeps us free from the influences of sin by **"<u>continually</u>"** heating us through his Word, energizing his Spirit....the power within us.

Just as a balloon is kept "hot" by regularly and frequently turning on the burner, man is kept "hot" by **<u>regularly and frequently</u>** turning on the power within him, which is done by studying, praying, and meditating on God's Word.

Therefore, for man to overcome his natural tendencies to cool and descend back into his sinful nature, the presence of God's power within man must be the continual source of power that keeps him "hot and aloft" through his daily "flight through life."

8] Falling vs. Descending

Unlike an airplane that can glide at a constant rate during its descent, a balloon is either flying or falling, and will descend at an accelerated rate as it cools. As the balloon cools, it can begin to descend so slowly that it will not be easily perceived. However, that rate can increase dramatically to several hundred feet a minute in a matter of seconds. One minute the balloon can be floating quietly through the sky, the next, it can be virtually falling like a parachute. Therefore, flying a balloon demands constant vigilance.

When a pilot wants to descend, he must fly the balloon to a lower altitude. He does this by allowing the air within the balloon to cool to less than what would be necessary to sustain level flight. However, he must then maintain that lower temperature to keep that rate of his descent constant.

Because a balloon is so large, it does not respond rapidly to any change in its flight characteristics. Therefore, change must be anticipated and initiated before it is needed. Generally, it takes several seconds for a balloon to react to any change. If change is not initiated until it is needed, by the time the balloon responds, it could be too late, especially at lower altitudes where there are obstacles like power-lines.

The Bible tells us that we are either "walking in the Spirit" or "walking in the flesh." Similar to a balloon, man is either "flying like an eagle," or he is "falling." Man does not "glide" in his descent, he falls! The Bible refers to this as "back-sliding." Also, like a balloon, that descent begins subtly but increases rapidly until he is in a downward plunge spiritually. Once that fall begins, it is difficult to stop. Therefore, spiritual decay must be anticipated, and constant vigilance must be maintained through studying God's Word, praying, and meditation on Christ's teachings to prevent it from occurring.

The Bible tells us that if we...
"Walk in the Spirit, we will not fulfill the lusts of the flesh." Galatians 5:16

The influences of sin are all around us, and like gravity, they are constantly "pulling" at us. If we are to maintain our freedom from these influences, we must constantly keep our spirits "hot." We can do this by maintaining a close, personal relationship with the one who can lift us above sin's control, Jesus Christ, the WORD of God.

Arise Fly High Float Free • 17

9] The Power of Heated Air

The average balloon can weigh somewhere around one hundred and fifty to two hundred pounds depending on its size. The larger commercial balloons used to carry up to a dozen or more passengers can weigh several hundred pounds. Some of the special shape balloons that are constructed to resemble some object or character can weigh even more.

The basket which hangs under the balloon carries the flight instruments, the fuel tanks, the fuel load, and can weigh well over three hundred pounds. When passengers are added, the total balloon can weigh upwards of a thousand pounds or considerably more. This is a significant amount of weight, and when you consider that it is lifted by only heated air, you can begin to appreciate the power of that force.

Talk to any Christian and you will probably hear stories of a person who, in their earlier life, was very worldly and living a very sinful lifestyle. We may tend to take these stories lightly and think they are exaggerated for dramatic effect. We simply do not have an appreciation for the "lifting capacity" of God's Grace. It can change a person from one who is weighed down by personal issues and transform him into someone who can "float" above the pull of those forces that once controlled his life.

The Bible refers to the force that distributes God's Grace as his "Spirit." In the Old Testament, the Hebrew word for God's Spirit is "ruwach" [roo'akh] and simply means wind, by resemblance of a breath of air. This word is simply translated in other areas of the Bible as "air." In the New Testament the Greek word for God's Spirit is "pneuma" [pnyoo'mah]. It also refers to a simple current of air, i.e. a breath or a breeze. Thus, both of these words refer to a similar concept.

These ancient people appreciated the power of air as it controlled the weather and propelled their ships across the sea for great distances. Therefore, when they needed a word to describe the enormous power of God's influence on a person they chose a word that conveyed potential, authority, control, strength, mastery, rule, influence, dominion, force and... Power!

God's Spirit, like air, is both invisible and has great power. It does not matter how much sin weighs a person down; God's grace is sufficient to overcome any load.

"Jesus saves" is not a phrase to be taken lightly

10] Straight and Level Flight

The first flight technique a student is taught in a balloon [or airplane] is straight and level flight. It is described as the constant correction for any ascent or descent of the aircraft which occurs during flight. Its purpose is to maintain a predetermined altitude. A balloon in flight is in a constant state of change. It is either cooling or being heated by the pilot. As it cools it falls, as it is heated it rises. Because of the balloon's mass, it responds to these changes slowly. Once change begins, momentum takes over, and it is difficult to stop. Thus, any changes in the aircraft's flight characteristics must be anticipated, and forces must be applied to control them <u>before they begin</u>.

The primary goal of an instructor in teaching a student to fly a balloon is to help him learn to anticipate change. Once change occurs and the balloon begins to fall, it is difficult to stop. A balloon which is falling must first be heated to the point of equilibrium again to stop the fall. This can take from several seconds to a minute or more. The amount of time needed depends on the size of the balloon and the amount of air needed to be heated, as well as the temperature of the air within it at that particular time. Once the fall is stopped, the balloon must be reheated above this state to regain lift and return it to the altitude it was at before the unintended decent. Thus, a strong, long, burn is needed. Therefore, it should be evident that regaining the initial altitude of the balloon can take some time.

An experienced balloon pilot can actually feel the balloon cool and begin to fall before it actually does so. Before a student can attain his private pilot's license, they must learn to anticipate these negative changes and maintain the balloon within one hundred feet of a predetermined altitude. The margin of control for a commercial pilot is reduced to only fifty feet. While this may sound like a large margin of error, it is not. Considering

that even a small balloon stands nearly seventy feet tall, this margin of error is actually only slightly more than half of the balloon's total height. A balloon can fall at nearly a thousand feet a minute or over ten times its total height. A lapse of concentration can put the pilot into the ground before he has time to recover. An experienced balloon pilot can actually maintain his altitude in terms of inches.

Much like a balloon in flight, our Christian walk is a state of constant change. We are both a product of our old human nature and the new nature of Christ's Spirit within us. Thus, we are under the constant state of influence by both the forces of God's Grace and our natural sinful nature. Both forces exert their pull on us, trying to influence our choices and affect the outcome of our decisions. The Bible tells us that we have control over these forces in our lives. "If we walk in the Spirit we will not fulfill the lusts of the flesh." [Galatians 5:16] By remaining in constant contact with God through His Word, prayer, and meditation, we remain "hot" and overcome the pull of sin in our lives. However, if we neglect God's Word, seldom pray or consider Christ's teachings, we allow ourselves to "cool" spiritually and quickly come under the ever-present influences of the pull of sin. Once we start a downward plunge, momentum takes over and it is difficult to stop. Only a strong blast of God's Grace can overcome this rapid "cooling," once again, "heating" us and enabling us to rise above the pull of our earthly, sinful desires.

Oh Lord, you have promised to "work in us both to desire and perform your will." [Philippians 2:13] You have told us that "we can have confidence, that He who has begun a good work within us, will continue it until we are safely home in His loving arms." [Philippians 1:6] Therefore, we humbly ask that you keep us "hot" for you, and give us victory today by your Word and your Spirit, so we can overcome those things in our lives that would pull us away from you and back into the sinful practices you saved us from.

11] Not Hot Enough

Occasionally a balloon will be used to attract attention at some commercial venture or during a public event. This is referred to as a "stand-up." During these events the air in the balloon is simply heated enough to lift the weight of the balloon itself, but not enough to lift the total weight of the aircraft [basket, tanks, fuel and pilot]. This causes the balloon to stand erect, displaying its size, color, and elegance, but no flight activity occurs. The pilot's responsibility is to simply keep the balloon hot enough to remain in an upright position, but not hot enough to actually fly.

I have done many of these events over the years. They tend to be somewhat boring as the balloon is intended to fly and not sit on the ground. However, occasionally people will approach the balloon and ask some questions regarding its construction or operation. After a short conversation, most remark how they would love to take a flight in a balloon someday, but rarely express a desire to simply stand in one when it is inflated and sitting on the ground. Just as the person who constructed the balloon intended it to fly high above the pull of earth's gravity, God intends for Christians to soar high above the pull of their sinful nature.

As a pilot, I have always been interested in any type of flying. Many years ago, before the Federal Aviation Administration required ultra-light pilots to have a license, I went to a "fly-in" of some ultra-light airplanes. As I drove up to the field where the event was held, I became excited by the site of several colorful airplanes, all positioned in a straight line along a cleared, grassy landing strip. After parking my car, I walked along a line of about a dozen airplanes examining their construction and colorful designs. Beside each aircraft stood a pilot with his sunglasses, chronograph "pilot's watch" and clipboard. Other planes were taxing up and down the runway, but none were actually flying?

After spending some time watching the planes taxi back and forth across the field, I asked one pilot when the planes would fly. He informed me that everyone there was learning to fly and no one actually flew yet. He further explained that occasionally a pilot would start his plane and taxi it up and down the runway to learn to control the aircraft. With time that pilot would taxi faster and faster until the airplane would attain lift and flight, if only for a second or two. The pilot would then cut the power and settle back to earth, which was their equivalence to learning to land.

Apparently, with experience, the periods of "flight" would increase in length until sustained flight would be attempted. I asked how many of the pilots in attendance had actually flown beyond a few seconds and he replied, "None!" He then asked me if I would be interested in getting involved in the group and learn to fly. I took out my commercial and instructor pilot certificates, showed them to him and left. The excitement I felt as I approached the field turned into disappointment. Although the airplanes looked exciting, I had no desire to just drive one up and down the runway. I wanted to fly!

All the individuals in attendance of that event that morning had all the "stuff" a real pilot needed. They looked the part, knew the terms, and talked the talk, they even had an airplane! However, none of them flew beyond a few short seconds. Each week people come to churches throughout this country. They seek answers on how they might escape the "gravity" of their sinful nature and soar in freedom above their depression and destructive desires. However, they meet people who are just like the "pilots" at that airfield I visited so long ago. People who look like Christians, talk like Christians, and even have a Bible like Christians, but have never really "flown" above the sinful desires that hold them down.

A balloon is made to fly and any other function it may serve is generally anticlimactic and diminishes its magnificence. The same is true for a Christian. God created us to rise up above the everyday cares of life. We should be like eagles that sore over the turbulent winds that surround their habitat. We were made to "shine" like lights in a dark and decaying world so our brilliance can attract others to the source of our power…. God. To live any other way is to diminish the power of God in our lives and reduces the attractiveness of an existence that should display enormous potential, a peacefulness that is beyond understanding and a joy that is generated by a personal relationship with our creator.

12] When A Balloon becomes a Sail

A balloon is a huge object. When someone sees one up close for the first time, they usually walk over to the opening at the bottom of the envelope, and staring up into the structure they remark, "Wow, it sure is big." Balloons come in various sizes. The average balloon you will see floating through the sky holds over 70,000 cubic feet of super-heated air, stands nearly 80 feet tall, and 60 feet wide. Some balloons can be as large as 200,000 cubic feet or more.

I've heard it said that the average-sized balloon is big enough to hold the contents of eleven eighteen wheeler trailers. Whether that is true or not, the simple fact is, a balloon is R-E-A-L-L-Y BIG! When fully inflated, the average balloon can easily lift well over a half-ton, carrying the basket, fuel, tanks, pilot, and passengers.

It takes a lot of fabric to construct these gentle giants. When fully inflated, they are a majestic sight to behold and can attract a lot of attention. In the hands of a skilled pilot, they can safely and gently navigate over distances of ten miles or more to a small, predetermined landing site. When operated under certain guidelines and specific weather conditions, ballooning is very safe. However, due to the size of the aircraft, certain weather conditions can present a very real danger to those in or around the aircraft, both in the sky and on the ground.

One of the dangers of ballooning while it is still on the ground is "dishing." As the balloon is inflated, heated air presses against the sides and top of the envelope. This constant pressure keeps the fabric tight, giving the balloon its characteristic oval appearance. When in flight, the balloon easily maintains its shape due to the amount of upward pressure it takes to produce lift. However, while on the ground, the pressure against the top and sides of the balloon is significantly less.

As the balloon is allowed to cool after a flight, the fabric's inner pressure diminishes proportionately and the fabric along the sides of the aircraft becomes very loose as the balloon begins to deflate. During this stage, a gentle breeze of less than ten miles an hour can collapse the balloon's side, making it resemble a large bowl standing on its side. This is referred to as "dishing." Even on a relatively calm day, an occasional gust of wind can significantly dish the side of a balloon.

While on the ground, it is the pilot's primary responsibility to keep the balloon properly inflated and under control. He does this by maintaining the air in the balloon at a temperature sufficient to produce enough inner pressure to keep the balloon's sides tight, but not enough to cause lift. If the pilot is distracted and the balloon is allowed to cool too much, a simple gust of wind could collapse the balloon's side, causing it to "dish."

Dishing makes the balloon vulnerable to two significant dangers. The first danger is the possibility of burning a hole in the balloon. While properly inflated, the sides of the balloon are kept sufficiently away from the flame as the pilot regularly heats the aircraft, keeping it HOT. If the gust of wind causes the balloon to dish, the side of the balloon may collapse enough to where it is directly above the burner. If the pilot "blasts" the burner, he will burn a hole in the balloon, rendering it unsuitable for flight.

The second danger of dishing is the possibility of the balloon becoming deformed enough to become a sail. As the side of the balloon collapses, it catches the wind. Depending on the strength of the gust, the balloon can be blown over and onto an object close by, possibly tearing the otherwise delicate fabric. A gust of wind can also cause the balloon to drag across the ground and into surrounding objects, damaging the aircraft and possibly injuring anyone near it.

In a similar way, Christians can be adversely affected by occasional circumstances which cause them to cool and become vulnerable to a deformation of their continence, altering their outward witness for Christ. In the Gospel of Matthew, it is written that...

"You are the light of the world. A city on a hill cannot be hidden. Neither do people light a lamp and put it under a bowl. Instead they put it on its stand, and it gives light to everyone in the house. In the same way, let your light shine before men, that they may see your good deeds and praise your Father in heaven." Matthew 5:14-16

It could take years to develop a strong Christian witness and only a few seconds to destroy it. The solution? .... keep "hot" by daily, constant communication with God [prayer]; ...reading daily devotionals from respected pastors and authors; ...hide God's Word in your heart by practicing daily memorization techniques; ...maintain frequent Christian fellowship through weekly worship and other methods of contact; ...maintaining a daily "quiet time" before the start of your day; ...all of which will help the Christian to stay "HOT" both "in" and "by" God's Holy Spirit.

13] False Lift

After arriving at a launch site, a balloon is taken out of its carrying bag and laid out on the ground. It is then filled with cold air by a large fan. Once it is fully inflated, the air in the balloon is heated by a burner, causing it to rise to an upright position. It takes only a minute or two to heat the balloon enough to stand erect. Depending on the balloon's size, it can take much longer to heat it sufficiently to attain enough temperature to allow it to fly. During this time, a balloon pilot must be aware of a potentially dangerous situation called false lift.

False lift is a phenomenon which occurs when a moderate breeze blows across the top of a balloon causing lift. The top of an inflated balloon is gently rounded, resembling the top of an aircraft wing. As air moves across it, lift can be generated like air moving across an airplane's wing. Since the top of a balloon is very large, it takes only a relatively gentle gust of wind to produce enough lift to raise the balloon off the ground.

False lift can be mistaken for the true lift that results from the heated air within the balloon. During the inflation process, the pilot must be very aware of the difference between the two. Depending on the weight of the balloon, wind speeds of as little as eight miles per hour can possibly exert enough lift to raise the balloon off the ground before the air within it is heated enough to sustain that lift. Once the balloon lifts off and begins to move with the wind, its forward motion will quickly match the relative speed of the wind blowing across its top, causing the false lift to cease. The balloon will then descend into some obstacle beneath it before the pilot has enough time to compensate for and reverse the effect.

In the book of Ephesians, the apostle Paul wrote about the dangers of works replacing God's Grace as a perceived means of salvation. Two thousand years later, we still deal with the misunderstanding that we are not saved by our good works, we are saved by God's grace which is freely given and not the results of anything we do [Ephesians 2:8-9]. However, the presence of God's Grace within us results in good works which we perform for the Glory of God. It has been said that...

"Grace is the root of salvation, while good works are the fruit of salvation."

Too often people have mistakenly believed that they could work their way to heaven by being good. They have allowed their actions to give them a sense of "false lift" towards God. However, when it was needed most, that inner feeling of self-worth was not sufficient to sustain them through some trial, or the pull of their corrupt nature towards some passionate, personal desire. There is a vast difference between the invisible power of God

within a man, and man's desire to be good and perform some noble act in the name of God.

"Not everyone who says to me, 'Lord, Lord,' will enter the kingdom of heaven, but only he who does the will of my Father who is in heaven. Many will say to me on that day, 'Lord, Lord, did we not prophesy in your name, and in your name drive out demons and perform many wonderful works?' Then I will tell them plainly, 'I never knew you. Away from me, you evildoers!' Matthew 7:21-23

14] Choices

Air blankets the earth in layers. These layers generally move in different directions and at different speeds. As a balloon ascends through these layers, it travels in the direction and speed of the air layer it is in. However, because of the sheer size of a balloon, as it ascends from one layer into another, it is not uncommon for the top of the balloon to be in one layer of air and be influenced by its speed and direction of travel, while the bottom of the aircraft will be in the other layer, and under the influence of its speed and direction of travel. Any significant difference in the speed and direction of these two layers of air can adversely affect the balloon's flight characteristics, as the effects of one layer will tend to overcome the effects of the other. Therefore, the pilot must choose to ascend or descend into one layer or the other. That choice is usually influenced by the speed and direction of a particular layer of air and its effect on the pilot's intended destination. Where the balloon ultimately concludes its flight is directly dependent on the pilots' choices during the flight. Therefore, choice affects outcome.

Some pilots fly in areas of the country where they can travel in any direction safely. However, I fly in an area populated with two major cities separated by a winding river, two large lakes, three major airports [one being a restricted military base], all surrounded by large wooded areas. Landing sites are at a premium and each flight is directed towards an intended target. I do not have the luxury of aimlessly drifting through the sky. I plan my flights before they are made and maintain a constant focus during the flight on my intended landing site. It has made me a better pilot and has sharpened my skills of navigating the balloon through the ever-changing currents of air in which I fly.

The Bible tells us that: "If we follow God's instructions, we will not gratify the desires of our sinful nature. For our sinful nature desires what is opposed to God's Spirit within us, and God's Spirit within us is opposed to our sinful nature! These two forces are in constant conflict with each other, making it very difficult for us to do what is right in the eyes of God!" [Galatians 5:16-17]

As we go through life, we are faced with constantly changing emotions and desires which influence our daily decisions. If our moral priorities are not well defined, we will tend to drift aimlessly from day to day making choices that may fulfill our natural desires but are in contrast to God's Spirit within us and his desires for us. When we find ourselves caught between these two opposing forces we must make a decision as to which one we will choose to follow. Choice effects outcome! We are responsible for the choices we make and must live with their consequences.

The decisions we make are strongly influenced by our values, priorities and true inner beliefs. God gives us his Spirit to help us make right choices [Philippians 2:13-14]; ...choices that will insure a proper outcome for us and others involved in, or affected by those choices; ...choices that will not lead to bad consequences; ...choices that will lead us safely through life and to the ultimate destination of a safe and gentle landing at the end of our "life-flight."

15] A Different Point Of View

As a pilot, I have always prided myself with a good sense of direction. For years my wife and I lived in the Western region of our city. We frequently utilized a major thoroughfare that we assumed took us directly to the Eastern portion of the city when we found it necessary to go there. We used this particular road because it appeared to be the most direct route and took the least amount of time. For ten years, I was under the impression that this road ran directly from West to East, until I flew over it one day and saw it from a different point of view.

While drifting slowly over the roadway during a summer's evening flight, I looked down to find that the road I had been traveling on for so many years was like an optical illusion. At one point, it actually headed true North before turning back to the East. Curious as to how I could have missed this fact, I further studied the route. I observed that at two intersections, the road deviated slightly to the North, changing travel direction. At two other busy areas, the road "ever-so-slightly" curved further to the North. These misleading areas were connected by sections of a straight running roadway, which gave the impression of "exactness" of the direction of travel. The conclusion of this surprising revelation was that while I did eventually end up East of where I began, I was considerably further North than if I had traveled to the East in a straight line.

Looking down from above, I was able to see the route in its entirety, giving me an understanding of how the busyness of the intersections distracted from the subtle changes in direction, and the straightness of the other sections of the roadway fooled me into assuming the road was something it was not, a straight connection between two points without deviation. I was surprised to learn how clutter and activity could be enough of a distraction to give one an improper sense of direction. This lesson taught me to always rely on my compass and not on my "perceived" good sense of direction.

In his first letter to Timothy, Paul instructs the young disciple to faithfully attend to three things until he returned, "reading, exhortation, and doctrine." [1 Timothy 4:13]. Paul understood how "busyness" and lack of priorities can clutter a person's life, leading them in the wrong direction in their Spiritual development. Paul also warned of men who would come into the young church with subtle changes to the gospel of Christ, giving the impression of truth. However, their false teachings would subtly lead in a different direction away from God's Word, causing one to eventually arrive at conclusions far from what God intended.

We cannot assume that just because a road states out in a particular direction, it will continue in that direction, or that it will ultimately take us to the place where we intended to go. We must be constantly aware of any subtle changes in direction, lest we be led off of our intended course. This is particularly true regarding the Word of God. There are those who pervert God's Word, leading us away from the path of truth for their personal gain. At first they may appear to be genuine, but they deviate from truth, ever-so-slightly, leading us further and further away from where God intended us to ultimately be. In His Word, God warns us of such, and promises to lead us on the right path if we remain in His Word and use it as our ultimate compass to guide us through life.

"Your ears shall hear a word behind you, saying, "This is the way, walk in it," Whenever you turn to the right hand or whenever you turn to the left." Isaiah 30:21 [NKJV]

16] The Attracting Power Of A Balloon

During my early years of flying balloons, I attended several regional balloon rallies. I was always amazed by the number of people who were attracted to these events. The most popular part of the weekend always seemed to be the balloon glow. A balloon glow is an evening event that occurs after dark. The balloons remain on the ground. The burners are periodically fired, illuminating the interior of the envelope against the dark night sky, dramatically displaying the balloon's colorful majesty.

I frequently come across people who express no interest in ever flying in a balloon but love to see them displayed. Balloons have been part of our city now for over thirty years. People will still pull over to the side of the road to watch one float by on a beautiful, clear morning or evening flight. Thousands still come out to watch the balloons light up a night sky when area balloonists occasionally get together for some local event. This illustrates one undeniable fact, balloons attract attention and can draw a crowd.

Jesus Christ, the living Son of God said, "if I be lifted up, I will draw all men to me." [John 12:32]. For over two thousand years, Jesus Christ has been the center of interest all over this planet. Despite our regional and cultural differences, monuments to him have been erected on virtually every continent and in every country the world over. Though there are those who express no interest in him on a day-to-day basis, when a crisis occurs, they instinctively turn to him for comfort.

Jesus Christ has been part of our national heritage for over two hundred years now. Each week millions across this country still take one morning out of their busy week to come together and celebrate his majesty and glory. Despite what you might personally think of him, these facts illustrates one undeniable truth, Jesus Christ attracts attention and can draw a crowd like no one else in the history of mankind.

17] The Man Who Would Not Look Up

One morning as I was maneuvering my balloon into an intended landing site, I slowly floated over the tree tops which surrounded the area. Looking down, I noticed a man on the side of the road about a hundred feet below me. He slowly walked along with his hands in his pockets. His head was slumped forward like a man with a burden on his mind. I called down to him, "Good morning," but he did not respond. Thinking he did not hear me I called again, "Good morning." Again, there was no response, so I yelled a little louder, "Helloooo!" The man stopped and looked around, but when he saw no one, he simply continued walking. Finally, I yelled, "Up here!" Again the man stopped. He looked side to side, …turned around, …then looked side to side again. Still seeing no one, he continued on his way. I could not get the man to look up.

The balloon eventually passed over him and settled into a field which was separated from the man by a wide stand of trees and beyond his line of sight. He had missed the opportunity to see the beautiful balloon slowly floating above him. He never knew that I was up there. Who knows if the sight of the balloon passing overhead that morning might have given that man something other to consider then what was on his mind? Who knows if that experience might have lifted his spirit as it usually for many who happen to come upon the colorful gentle giant and witnessed its awesome presence as it unexpectedly passed through their everyday existence? Who knows what effect it might have had on that man that morning? For many years I pondered the question of why that man didn't look up on that morning so long ago. I have come to this conclusion: possibly, he didn't look up because he didn't expect to see anything up there!

I occasionally think of that man as I pass through life and see people who are hurting. I wonder how many times God, through some person or experience, tries to call down to them, but they simply won't "look up." It is possibly that they don't look up for the same reason that man so long ago didn't either; …they don't expect anyone to be up there! They miss the opportunity to know that someone is up there looking down on them; …someone who cares; …someone who loves them; …someone who sent his Son to die for their sins; …someone who wants to give them joy, peace and abundant life now and for eternity. If only they would "look up."

What about you? Are you like that man who would not "look up?" Has life got you so weighted down that you cannot "look up?" Knowing that I am a balloon pilot, people occasionally ask me if the balloons are still flying in the area. I reply that they are still flying, but you will never see them unless you look for them, and since they fly in the sky, you will have to "look up" to see them. The same is true for God. He is still answering prayer, providing peace and joy, offering comfort and encouragement through His Spirit. However, if you want to experience all of these blessings, much like the balloon, you will have to stop what you are doing and "look up."

My voice you shall hear in the morning, O LORD; In the morning I will direct it to you, and I will look up. Psalm 5:3

18] All For A Loaf Of Bread

On New Years' Day, 1992, I was doing an afternoon flight for a man and his wife. I remember the day as having gentle winds with a grey, high overcast sky and pleasant temperatures in the high fifties. We slowly drifted over the city, finally coming to a potential landing site in the large backyard of a private residence. I called my chase crew on the radio and instructed them to ask the land-owner for permission to land the balloon on his property. Permission was given by an elderly man who came out in a tattered coat and quietly watched as we landed, deflated, and packed up the balloon.

During the process, some of the man's neighbors walked over to his yard to watch the activity. One by one they approached the man, wished him a "happy new year" and joined him in watching the crew as they packed up the balloon. After all, how often does anyone have a hot air balloon land in their backyard? Soon his yard was filled with his excited neighbors, and there was joyful activity everywhere. I occasionally looked over to the property owner and noticed a large smile on his face. He obviously enjoyed being surrounded by all of the friendly activity on an otherwise dull and average day.

After packing up the equipment, I handed the man a color picture of the balloon. I signed my name to it and thanked him for his hospitality. It was apparent by his reaction that the picture would be a wonderful reminder of a treasured memory. As we were preparing to leave, we said our goodbye's to the many people who continued to stand around visiting with each other and the elderly gentleman. It was then that a car pulled into the driveway and up to the house. A woman exited the vehicle holding a small brown paper bag and walked over to the elderly man. Although I could not hear their conversation, it was evident that she was asking what all activity was about. The man pointed to us, where the balloon landed in the yard, and the picture I had given him. The woman looked at the picture, then threw the bag on the ground and stormed into the house.

Concerned that we had created a problem, I approached the man and asked if everything was alright. He chuckled and replied, "Yes," as he bent over to pick up the bag the woman had thrown down. As he lifted it, I noticed that it contained a loaf of bread. He told me that the woman was his wife. Apparently, being bored earlier in the afternoon, she selfishly decided to leave her husband home alone and go shopping. By doing so, she missed the entire event. Her loss was compounded by the fact that she loved watching the balloons float over their home and frequently expressed a desire to be near one and learn more about them. She missed her opportunity, as well as the joy of seeing and interacting with her neighbors, ...all for a loaf of bread.

The Bible tells us that Jesus will come back to earth someday for his own and strongly suggests that we patiently wait for Him with great expectations. Some think this is foolish, while others live their life in such a way that they are ready day by day if he should appear.

You can spend your whole life waiting for a balloon to land in your yard, and it may never happen. However, consider what a loss it would be for a balloon to land in your yard, and you miss it for a simple loaf of bread. If I had a large back yard which was located in an area where balloons frequently passed overhead, and I was interested in having one land in it, I would probably keep it nicely mowed, and on days when the winds were gentle, and the sun was shining, you would probably find me sitting out there in a lawn chair during the hours I knew the balloons flew.

"Don't neglect church and meetings with other believers, but encourage each other to be faithful, especially now that the day of Christ's coming back again is drawing near." Hebrews 10:25 [The Living Bible]

19] Where am I???

The Global Positioning System, otherwise known as a G.P.S., has become an indispensable piece of equipment to a pilot who must constantly be aware of his exact location. Its value increases if that pilot is traveling in poor weather conditions, with limited visibility, and at night! The G.P.S. can give the pilot his exact location anywhere in the world to within a few feet radius of error. It also provides information regarding direction, speed of travel, estimated time of arrival to a point of reference, altitude, and position in regards to a point of reference. It also provides directional assistance to get back on course if you get off course. It does all these things by aligning itself with three or more satellites, and then triangulating its exact location by comparing it with the positioning of the satellites in space to which it is aligned.

Obviously, the practicality of this object varies in direct proportion to the user's needs. However, knowing your exact location can be very important to people other than pilots who are navigating an aircraft through the sky. It is easy to know where you are when surrounded by familiar points of reference. However, if you take an individual out of their usual surroundings, they can quickly become disoriented and lost. Knowing your location is essential to determining the direction you must go to get you back to familiar surroundings.

The G.P.S. can help a father piloting the family car by providing its exact location while traveling in a strange town. It can help a sportsman find the exact location of his favorite fishing hole in the middle of a large lake where there are otherwise no points of reference. It can assist a hiker lost in the wilds to determine his exact location and needed direction and distance to a known point of reference, such as a ranger station. It can provide the information to rescue authorities regarding a motorist's location awaiting assistance due to a mechanical breakdown on some deserted roadway. It can also serve a life-saving function by communicating the exact location of a rescue worker to the pilot of a medical evacuation helicopter during an instance where time is crucial. Will you ever own one of these things? In reality, you already do. It is called a Bible.

The Bible is "God's Positioning System." Like the regular G.P.S., the Bible can determine your exact location in life by triangulating with three points of reference, …the Father, Son, and Holy Spirit. Once you know your position in reference to the Heavenly Triune, the Bible can point you in the proper direction of travel towards God. It is an indispensable tool to those who are "lost" and need to be "saved." It can tell you how far off course you are and the direction you need to turn to get back on course. It can tell you how far you've come, …how far you have to go, …and can even tell you your "spiritual elevation" [or how close to God you are] throughout your journey.

20] Where am I going?

A balloon can only fly in one direction, ...with the wind. Therefore, before a pilot can determine where he will fly on any given day, and if a safe flight can be made, he must find out in which direction the wind is traveling, its speed and if any changes in the weather are expected during the flight.

This information is received from two sources. First, the pilot takes a few minutes to call the local flight service station. He receives information relative to the weather and flight operations in the general region in which he intends to fly. When the pilot decides if the weather over that area will allow him to conduct a safe flight, he can proceed to the next step in his pre-flight planning.

A balloon flight usually occurs over an area of ten miles or less. The pilot uses a small, toy balloon filled with helium to determine the exact speed and direction of the winds in the specific area where his flight will occur. This balloon is referred to as a "Pibal," which is short for "pilot balloon." As the balloon is released, the pilot watches its speed and direction of travel as it ascends upward. It will not only tell him the direction in which he will fly, but by estimating the speed of the balloon he can determine how far he will travel during his flight that day. As the balloon ascends, the pilot can also learn if the wind's speed or direction changes at higher altitudes. This information allows the pilot to choose a launch site that will best take advantage of these atmospheric factors and safely conduct his flight to a predetermined destination.

Each morning we look forward to ever-changing and unknown factors that can influence our attitude and the decisions we make that day. Taking a few minutes to plan our day is as essential for us as it is for a pilot to plan his flight. As Christians, we depend on God's Spirit to carry us through our day, just as the wind carries a balloon through its flight. Therefore, it just makes sense to take a few minutes each morning before we begin our day to send up a spiritual "pibal." By spending a few minutes reading God's Word and in prayer, we can look to God to guide us on our journey through the day [as well as through our life] to a predetermined destination.

"Your word is a lamp to my feet and a light for my path." Ps 119:105

21] Hello, ...Is Anyone Out There?

Whenever I fly, I maintain constant communication with my chase crew on the ground, giving them regular updates on my location and direction of flight. Depending on my location, I also maintain constant communication with the control tower of one of the three airports located in the area in which I live. The control tower provides information regarding any commercial or general aviation traffic which may be operating in my flight area. The tower then alerts that traffic to my altitude and direction of flight. This exchange of information is essential for avoiding any close encounters which can turn what would have been a pleasant day of ballooning into a bad experience for everyone.

Different aircraft types tend to travel at different speeds and altitudes. Constant communication between them is necessary to avoid potential conflicts. Communications during flight operations can be classified into two categories: coordination and control. Coordination conveys the intentions of the pilots operating together in a given airspace. Control comes from an agency responsible for the coordination of flight operations in a given area.

Three things are necessary to maintain good communications during a flight: ...the radio must be turned on, ...the radio must be tuned to the proper frequency, ...the radio operator must be listening. Without these three necessary factors you are all alone and very vulnerable while in the air.

Good communication is as essential on the ground as it is in the air. As we go through life, each of us is traveling at different speeds and in different directions. Unless we are careful, we can easily come into conflict with those around us. A constant exchange of information allows us to prevent confrontations with those we interact with.

Each day we are surrounded by many different trials and temptations which can disrupt our lives to varying degrees if we are not prepared for them. Keeping in constant communication with God is like having a controlling agency to alert us to potential dangers that surround us and direct us away from them. Whether we are trying to interact with those around us, or are looking to God for some direction in life, the three necessary factors for good communication apply:

- You need to be turned on by God's Grace,
- You need to be tuned into his Spirit,
- And you need to be listening.

"And your ears shall hear a word behind you, saying, "This is the way, walk in it," when you turn to the right or when you turn to the left." Isaiah 30:21-22

22] FAR 91:103 - Conducting a "Pre-flight

All aviation activity is regulated by the Federal Aviation Administration, otherwise referred to as the FAA. Rules and regulations regarding aviation are published in the Federal Aviation Regulations, otherwise referred to as the FAR's. The first rule a pilot learns as a student is FAR part 91:103. "Each pilot in command shall, before beginning a flight, familiarize himself with all available information concerning that flight." This rule is referred to by pilots as "conducting a pre-flight."

This rule applies to a pilot regardless of whether they are operating a powered aircraft or a balloon. Conducting a pre-flight includes investigating any and all possible factors that might affect the safe and orderly performance of an intended flight. It is said that the most important part of any flight occurs before the aircraft leaves the ground.

While there are no rules or laws regulating the preparation we should undergo before beginning our daily activities, there are many examples given to us by the lives of successful people, which demonstrate how they prepared before beginning their day. One outstanding example that comes to mind is the father of our country, George Washington. Many years ago I visited Mount Vernon, the home of this great man. While participating in an organized tour, our group passed through General Washington's personal study. The man conducting the tour pointed to a set of stairs that entered the room from the rear and connected the study to second story of General Washington's home where his bedroom was located. The man told us that each morning General Washington would begin his day very early [four O'clock I believe he said]. Using his finger, the man illustrated the path our first president would take across the room to a small piece of furniture containing a bible. Apparently General Washington began each day on his knees in prayer and studying God's Word. The man then looked at us and said, "You are standing in the room where much of what this country is today was conceived by General Washington while on his knees conversing with God."

Other examples of successful people who spent much time preparing for their day are King David and Jesus Christ himself. When I was first introduced to Jesus Christ as my personal Lord and Savior, I met a man who asked me if I had a morning "quiet time." before beginning my day. I told him that I didn't know what a "quiet time" was. When he described what he was referring to, I replied, "Oh, ...that"'s just like conducting a Pre-flight."

23] Tethered Flight

The primary purpose of a balloon is to float freely beyond the pull of gravity, high above the earth, riding on the wind and carrying its occupants above those obstacles far below to some distant location. The second most common function a balloon is used for is tethered flight. Tethering a balloon involves securing it to the ground by three ropes equally positioned around it. The ropes connected to the balloon prevent it from flying free or flying high. However, the restricted flight allows a large number of people the limited experience of finding out what riding in a balloon is like.

A tethered ride only lasts about four minutes. The balloon is heated and allowed to rise to the height of its restraining ropes, usually between only twenty or thirty feet above the ground. The balloon then quickly cools, settling back down on the ground again. While the occupants can momentarily experience lighter-than-air flight, it is far from what floating freely across the sky is really like. The short experience does not allow the individual to fully appreciate the true purpose for which the aircraft was created.

God created us to float freely through life. He intended us to be carried aloft by his Grace above the obstructions of sin that constantly pull at us from below and impedes our progress through life. However, just like the three restraining ropes that hold a balloon to the ground, the Bible tells us that there are three things that can hold us down and restrict our ability to experience the freedom God intended for us. They are: the lust of the flesh, the lust of the eye, and the pride of life. [1 John 2:15-16].

Many a Christian has missed the opportunity to "soar like eagles," because they have been shackled by their pride or their lust towards what they thought this life could offer them. They missed the chance to experience the peace of "flying free" and seeing things from God's point of view. Frequently during a tether operation, I jokingly threaten to cut the ropes and allow the balloon to fly away. Some people react quickly with fear demanding I not do that, while others express their desire to experience the freedom of untethered flight. Which one are you?

Have you ever wondered what it would like to be truly set free, ...free from worry, ...free from desire, ...free from anger, ...free from jealousy, ...free from fear? God tells us that this freedom is available to us, but it comes with a price. To experience true freedom, we have to separate ourselves from those things that hold us down and prevent us from moving away from where we are to where God intends to take us. We can either remain shackled to the ground, or we can....

...Arise,
...Fly High,
...Float Free.

"Those who live according to the flesh focus their minds on the things of the flesh, but those who live according to the Spirit, focus their minds on the things of the Spirit. For to be fleshly minded is death, but to be spiritually minded is life and peace." Romans 8:5-6

24] The Fuel Source

One of the necessary components of a Hot Air Balloon is its fuel source. Early balloons utilized fire to heat the air in the balloon. However, as they could not carry the fire with it, the balloon rose to only a small height, quickly cooled, and descended back to the earth. The flights were short and never traveled far from where they began. Today's balloons utilize propane as a fuel. The average balloon carries between twenty to thirty gallons of propane on each flight. However, the fuel capacity of a balloon can be much greater depending on the size of the balloon and the purpose of the flight. The propane is carried in aluminum or steel tanks secured to the sides of the basket. They allow the balloon to fly for hours with the potential of traveling great distances from where the flight began. When the propane runs out, the flight is over.

One of the necessary components of a Christian is the presence of God's Spirit in their life. It is the "fuel" that allows us to float freely above life's cares and the influences of those things that would pull us back to the lives we were set free from by God. The Bible tells us that God's Spirit is freely given to us by Faith [Ephesians 2:8-9]. However, the Bible also tells us that Faith is not something common to man; it is a gift and comes to us through God's Word. [Romans 10:17]

So, through God's Word comes faith, and through faith comes God's Grace, and through God's Grace comes God's Spirit, which is the power to both desire and perform God's will. Therefore, God's Word is the true fuel source that empowers us to raise above the pull of sin, just as the propane heats the balloon and allows it to rise above the pull of gravity.

As a balloon carries its fuel source with it, Christians should also carry their fuel source with them. We can do this by hiding God's word in our hearts through daily study, memorization, and meditation. If we do this God promises us that...

"...we would be like a tree which is planted by a river, which brings forth fruit in its season, and having plenty of water, its leaves do not wither." [Psalm 1:1-3]

"...no one would be able to stand before us all the days of our lives, for God would be with us, and He would make our way prosperous, for we would know and follow God's ways for us." [Joshua 1:5-9]

"...we would not be under the influence of sin." [Psalm 199:11]

"...we would be nourished and strengthened as a child is by it's mother's milk, allowing that child to grow and mature." [1 Peter 2:2]

"...we would not conform to the world's standards, but be transformed by the renewing of our minds." [Romans 12:1-2]

If we do not carry God's fuel source with us, our flight will be short and we will never really travel far from where it began.

25] The Mass Ascension

A hot air balloon rally may have anywhere from two dozen to over a hundred or more balloons in participation. A "mass ascension" occurs when all of the balloons inflate simultaneously, then launch into the sky in a blaze of fire and color. It is a spectacular sight to witness. However, almost immediately, you will notice an interesting phenomenon. Although launching together into the same air mass, the balloons will begin to separate. Some balloons will quickly climb to a higher altitude changing their direction and speed of travel. Others may remain closer to the ground. They may drift slowly and sometimes meander aimlessly in no particular direction. Though all the balloons launched from the same location and have no apparent means of directional control other than the wind that affected them all, still, they will all land several miles apart.

Although it is not a reliable constant, wind speed and direction tend to change with altitude. Therefore, the hotter a pilot heats the air in his balloon, the higher it will fly. As wind speed can increase with altitude, the higher a balloon flies, the faster and further it will travel during its flight.

I have met many people who claim to have committed their lives to the cause of Christ at an early age. Yet, they demonstrated a poor understanding of God's Word. Their attitude and character were not consistent with what one would expect from a Christian. In contrast, I have also met many who profess to have committed their lives to Christ for only a short time. Yet, they possessed an uncanny understanding of God's Word, and demonstrated a spiritual maturity which one would expect from a person who has spent many years following the principles of Christianity.

The Bible occasionally refers to an individual who has a zeal for God as being "hot," and one who is less concerned for the things of God as being "cold." [see Revelation 3:15]. Those who are "hot" tend to want to raise their awareness of Christ and have a closer walk with him. They spend much time in God's Word, prayer, and fellowship with other Christians. Since God is perceived to abide above, those who are more committed to the cause of Christ are said to have a "higher walk." They seem to travel further in their Christian walk than those who are "lukewarm" and simply play at Christianity when they find it convenient, or when necessary because of some adversity in their lives.

I contend that there are some similarities between the two above illustrations, and that the principles that govern them are the same. The "hotter" one is, the "higher" they fly, the faster they mature as a Christian and the further they will ultimately "travel" [or progress] over the course of their "flight" [or life's journey].

"Oh Lord, give us a passionate hunger for your Word. Light a fire in our hearts and guide us in our daily walk. Watch over us till we arrive at our ultimate destination with you at the end of our time here on earth."

26] The Invisible Power Within

This might sound strange but, on several occasions, people have actually approach my balloon, looked up into it and asked, "Where's the gas?" My answer always sounds somewhat sarcastic, but is accurate none-the-less; "Ahhhh, there is no gas, it is a "HOT-AIR" balloon…and air is invisible." They usually respond with a blank look and respond, "Oh," then they walk away a little embarrassed. Two things are immediately apparent here: we simply have no appreciation for the power of heated air, …and… we occasionally fail to realize that power is invisible.

Even after many years of flying these gentle giants, I sometimes am amazed at their ability to lift the amount of weight they do. However, I must continuously remind myself that it is not the balloon that is doing the lifting, but the <u>invisible power of the heated air inside of it</u> that does the lifting. Without that power, a balloon is as subject to the laws of gravity as any other object.

What makes a balloon unique is the capacity to harness that power and use it for a practical purpose. Uninflated, the balloon is nothing more than a pile of somewhere around twelve hundred yards of cloth. It is very heavy and must be carried about with great effort. Even when it is inflated with air, the balloon simply lays on its side, rolling around on the ground at the whim of the breezes that surround it. Only when the air within it is heated does it have the capacity to rise above the pull of gravity, fly high, and float freely through the sky.

We tend to classify people into two categories; "good" and "bad." We would be more accurate in stating that people have the capacity to be good or bad. What raises us above our bad or sinful nature is not ourselves, but the invisible power of Christ within us. When God "super-charges" our spirit with his Spirit, we receive that "invisible power" to rise above our sinful nature. Therefore, however you may see yourself, you can harness that invisible power that is placed within you by God. That power can make all the difference as to the type of person you can become, irrespective of the type of person you may now be.

27] Change

The concept of a balloon is really very simple. It is a somewhat oval sphere made of cloth that is filled with air. When the air is heated, it overcomes gravity and the cloth flies. However, what if you've never seen a balloon? Imagine a person pushing a wheel-barrel carrying a thousand yards of nylon. You walk up to the person and ask them what they intended to do with all that cloth. The person tells you they intend to make the cloth fly! ....Fly? You say to the person that they are crazy. Cloth doesn't fly, it falls like everything else. However, the person looks at you and tells you, "this cloth will fly." He then goes on his way, and you go yours thinking that the person you just met was crazy. Sometime later, you look up in the sky and see the person suspended from the cloth, floating effortlessly across the sky. How is that possible? The cloth was changed!!

We all know people who were once wild and living an undisciplined and self-destructive lifestyle. Then all of a sudden, they seem to have changed. Their priorities are different, their speech is different, they look different, act different. How it this possible? That person was changed!!

Many years ago I saw a movie called "The Planet of the Apes." Possibly you saw it also? For those who haven't, it was about an astronaut who is transported into the future where the earth is ruled by apes. In this futuristic world, the apes are intelligent and man is like a wild animal. The astronaut is captured and placed into a compound, much like our zoos today. He is placed with other humans who are undeveloped mentally and lack the ability to speak. As the humans are viewed much like we would view apes in one of our zoos, the astronaut's intelligence and ability to speak quickly singles him out as an anomaly to be studied. As the astronaut can talk and demonstrates intelligent, he displays two qualities all the other humans' lack, causing the apes to ask "how is this possible?"

In one scene, the astronaut is being questioned by an ape scientist. The astronaut tells of the world he comes from, a world of human intelligence. He also explains how he came to this planet ruled by apes, ...he flew! Of course the ape scientist doubts all he says. As the astronaut cannot prove the existence of this world he claims to come from, he takes a piece of ordinary paper, bends it into the shape of a paper airplane and sends it gliding across the room. The ape scientist is shocked as he has never seen an object fly. Again he asks: "How is this possible?"

How can an ordinary piece of paper fly? How can something that is ordinarily subject to the law of gravity defy that law? By changing! The Apostle Paul wrote: "It doesn't make any difference now whether we have been circumcised or not; what counts is whether we really have been changed into new and different people." Galatians 6:15 [TLB]

This concept of change is seen elsewhere, most notably in 2 Corinthians 5:17: "Therefore, if any man be in Christ, he is a new creature: old things are passed away; behold, all things are become new." [KJV]. In simple terms, that person was changed.

I have seen Christians who struggle with the question, "Have I really been saved?" I have heard preachers and good meaning individuals try to help these confused individuals obtain peace regarding this perplexing question by asking if they have ...prayed the prayer of faith? ...confessed Jesus as their Lord and Savior? ...walked the aisle and made a public profession? ...been baptized? While all of these actions may accompany a true conversion experience, none of them are proof of one. They all can easily be fabricated. The bible tells us that there is one unquestionable occurrence that can identify a true believer from one who was coaxed into making a decision under the duress of an emotional or traumatic incident, and that is "change!" Change is the only reliable proof that a person has truly been "Born Again."

Once again, consider the paper airplane in the above illustration. It is still constructed of the same material. Still, when it is configured differently, its characteristics change. It can then utilize that change to overcome a simple universal law, ...gravity! When the Holy Spirit of Christ enters a person, that person is changed. By that change, the "new creation" can now overcome another universal law, ...the law of sin.

"...for all have sinned and fall short of the glory of God," Romans 3:23-24

'So then, I myself in my mind am a slave to God's law, but in the sinful nature a slave to the law of sin." Romans 7:25

A pile of fabric can take on a new form and become something that is capable of performing things its previous form could not. Likewise, a person can be changed into a new creature capable of performing supernatural things their old self could not.

"I urge you therefore, brethren, by the mercies of God, to present your bodies as a living and holy sacrifice, acceptable to God, which is your spiritual service of worship. And do not be conformed to this world, but be <u>transformed [or changed]</u> by the renewing of your mind, that you may prove what the will of God is, that which is good and acceptable and perfect." Romans 12:1-2

28] All Things Being Equal

Equilibrium is the state of a balloon becoming equal to the weight of the air surrounding it. It's achieved when the pilot heats the air in the balloon and produces enough lift to equal the pull of gravity on the aircraft's total weight, but not enough to make the aircraft lighter than the air surrounding it. Although the total weight of the balloon may exceed a thousand pounds, when it is in this state, it can easily be lifted by one person and moved around on the ground. Essentially, it is in a state of weightlessness. However, to fly, the balloon must be further heated and become lighter than the air surrounding it.

When a pilot is preparing to take off on a flight, his first task is to inflate the balloon with a large gas powered fan. The fan blows cold air into the balloon and it slowly begins to inflate, rising up on its side. When the balloon is mostly full of cold air, the pilot heats the air in the balloon with the burner. As the air in the balloon is heated, it rises up till it is suspended above the basket and pilot beneath it.

To prevent the balloon from lifting off the ground in the event too much heat is applied, the pilot calls out to his crew to place their weight on the basket. This is accomplished by one or more crew members leaning on the sides of the basket with their arms. When the balloon is fully inflated and standing erect, the crew continues to exert their weight on the balloon basket to stabilize it as passengers begin to board the aircraft. Once all are on board, the pilot resumes heating the air within the balloon. After several seconds, the pilot will test the aircraft's buoyancy by calling out "weight off." The crew will remove their weight from the basket but will retain their grip on it, just in case it becomes necessary to stabilize it again. Once the balloon begins to demonstrate the ability to lift off, the pilot will call for the crew to let go completely to allow the aircraft to climb up and float freely into the sky.

When a balloon is filled with heated air it will naturally attempt to do what it was designed to do, fly! However, in the early stages of the inflation process, it can easily be held down by one or two of the crew. When a person is filled with God's Holy Spirit, they will naturally do what they were created to do, worship, and serve God. However, they can also be "held down" by one or two individuals who may attempt to prevent them from "flying away" from their old nature, and soaring freely with their new nature. Sometimes it might be necessary to tell your "crew"…"Weight off" to allow you to…arise, ….fly high, …and float free!

29] Be Ready, ...Always

On Christmas Eve 1992, I did a balloon flight over a small community in East Texas. I clearly remember the day as being a perfect day to fly. There was a high overcast, gentle Southeasterly winds, and pleasant temperatures. For about an hour, I slowly drifted over the landscape, eventually coming to rest in a large fenced-in field. I radioed my location to my crew and instructed them to request permission from the landowner to retrieve the balloon from his property before deflating it. Before long, I saw my crew drive up and approach the landowner's house. It didn't take long for my crew to receive permission to retrieve the balloon. The landowner even requested that he be allowed to help in the retrieval and pack-up.

Almost immediately, I saw an armada of people coming towards the balloon. Many were children excitedly running and screeching in delight. Within minutes I was surrounded by adults and children alike. People were taking pictures and posing beside the balloon as I kept it inflated until the chase vehicle arrived. When it did arrive, I told my crew to tie the balloon to the bumper. I wanted to express my appreciation to the landowner for his hospitality by giving those in attendance a tethered ride. I flew up and down with adults and their children until my fuel load was exhausted. Afterward, everyone took part in deflating and packing up the balloon and putting it into the chase vehicle.

As I was preparing to leave, I walked over to the landowner who appeared to be an elderly man in his eighties with a kind and generous face. I extended my hand to express my appreciation for his hospitality and thank him for allowing us to drive out onto his field to retrieve the balloon. With one arm around his wife, he extended his other arm and took my hand. As a tear ran down his face, he said, "No, ...Thank You!" He related to me that he was having a Christmas family reunion and that his family had not been together in some time. What a wonderful surprise it was to have a hot air balloon drop into the celebration. It was something they all would remember for the rest of their lives.

Many years ago, I had the privilege of hearing the great author and prophetic preacher Tim LaHaye speak about the second coming of Christ. He related how there are several hundred prophetic references to both the first and second coming of Christ. He mentioned how there are twice as many references regarding the second coming of Christ as the first. He stated that one hundred percent of the prophecies regarding Christ's first coming were fulfilled and asked what the probabilities were of that occurring? He then stated that if all the prophecies regarding

Christ's first coming were fulfilled, and there are twice as many regarding His second coming, it might be wise for us to be ready, always, because you never know when it might occur.

What are the possibilities of a hot air balloon landing in your yard, ...on Christmas Eve, ...during your family reunion? It can happen; it did to one East Texas family. You never know when it might happen to you. So, be ready...always!

30] Becoming Becalmed

Balloons characteristically fly in the morning from sunrise to two hours after sunrise and in the evening from two hours before sunset to sunset. This is because the wind which propels the balloon through the sky is generally at it gentlest during those times. A balloon pilot uses the wind as his mode of propulsion. If there is no wind, there is no movement, and the balloon will simply go up and come down exactly where it started its flight. If there is too much wind, the balloon becomes difficult to control, often resulting in a hard landing, increasing the possibility of injury to the occupants, or damage to the aircraft. A responsible pilot will take advantage of the best times of the day to fly when the wind is at its calmest close to the ground, but have movement at higher altitudes.

As the sun rises in the morning, it begins to heat the earth. This causes the air closest to the ground to also be heated, and it begins to rise. This is called convection. The air close to the ground is heated unequally due to geographical differences. Wooded areas heat slower than sandy or developed areas such as cities or towns. Also, large areas of water, such as rivers and lakes, tend to heat slower then wooded areas. Wind patterns begin to form and become more unpredictable as the sun gets higher in the sky. This makes controlling the balloon increasingly more difficult. Therefore, the pilot must take advantage of the calmer winds and fly before the convective activity of the sun begins.

As the sun begins to set in the evening, the heating effect it has on land begins to decrease, reducing the heating effect it has on the air. This can cause wind speeds to slow and possibly even stop. If the winds stop during a flight, the pilot loses maneuverability, and the only control he has is to go up or down. The balloon simply hangs suspended in the air by the hot air within it but is otherwise going nowhere. This is referred to as becoming "becalmed." It can present a serious problem depending on what the balloon is becalmed over. If a pilot is "becalmed," he tries to find winds at higher altitudes. If winds are found, the pilot can drift until he is over an acceptable landing site and then descend to a safe landing.

Just as wind is the "power factor" to a balloon, God's Holy Spirit is the "power factor" to the Christian. The heated air within a balloon enables it to rise above the pull of gravity and float freely in the sky above. The winds aloft provide it with maneuverability and allow the balloon to travel over great distances. Therefore, the air that fills it and the wind that propels it are the defining characteristics of a balloon. Without them, the sport of ballooning would not exist. Similarly, God's Spirit within a person allows that person to rise above the pull of sin and float freely above the influences of the many temptations that surround each of us every day. It is God's Spirit within us that allows us to persevere in adversity and perform tasks far above our natural abilities.

God's Spirit is the defining characteristic of a Christian. Without it, we as Christians cannot exist. God's Spirit gives us guidance and the ability to make good and successful decisions. It guides and propels us through life to a safe destination at the end of life and enables us to be a blessing to those whom we come in contact with.

In the original language the New Testament was written in [Greek], the word for "spirit" is "pneuma" (pnyoo'-mah).★ It refers to a current of air [i.e. breath or a breeze; by analogy or figuratively, a spirit].★ Just as a balloon needs the wind to fly and maneuver through its flight, a Christian needs God's Spirit to fly and maneuver through life. Without it, we become "becalmed," suspended in life, going nowhere, doing nothing.

He giveth power to the faint; and to them that have no might he increaseth strength. Even the youths shall faint and be weary, and the young men shall utterly fall: But they that wait upon the LORD shall renew their strength; **they shall mount up with wings as eagles**; they shall run, and not be weary; and they shall walk, and not faint. Isaiah 40:29-31 [NKJV]

★ (Biblesoft's New Exhaustive Strong's Numbers and Concordance with Expanded GreekHebrew Dictionary. Copyright (c) 1994, Biblesoft and International Bible Translators, Inc.)

31] The Balloon Glow

Seeing a group of colorful balloons floating across a cloudless, blue sky is indeed a glorious sight. However, it cannot compare to a group of balloons doing a "balloon glow." This is an event where balloons inflate after dark, allowing the fiery blast from their burners to illuminate them from the inside, accentuating the aircraft's color and magnificence.

The burners which power a hot air balloon are indeed engineering wonders. The power they emit is measured in British Thermal Units [BTU]. A BTU is the amount of energy needed to raise the temperature of one pound of water one degree Fahrenheit. Depending on its size, a burner can produce between twelve to twenty-four million BTU's an hour! The flame the burner emits can extend as long as eighteen feet, but only about one third to a half of the flame is usually visible.

Most balloons have a single burner. It is not uncommon for larger balloons to have two or more, which can produce an incredible amount of energy with a lifting capacity of several thousand pounds. A typical hot air balloon burner can heat the air in the top of the balloon to well over two hundred degrees Fahrenheit. Considering that water boils at 212 degrees Fahrenheit, one can appreciate that the air inside of a hot air balloon is really...HOT!

No matter the size or power of a burner, when it is ignited in the daytime, there is no visible change in the balloon's appearance. However, when it is ignited at night when the balloon is surrounded by darkness, the balloon's true brilliance shines forth. In the Gospel of Matthew, we read Jesus's commands regarding our character and how the world needs to see us.

"You are the light of the world. A city on a hill cannot be hidden. Neither do people light a lamp and put it under a cover. Instead they put it on its stand, and it gives light to everyone in the house. In the same way, let your light shine before men, that they may see your good deeds and praise your Father in heaven." Matthew 5:1416

I find it interesting that a balloon shines its brightest when it is surrounded by darkness. As Christians, we should do the same and shine the brightest when things are at their worst. It is then that we can let God's Spirit shine brightly through us, demonstrating the pure brilliance of God's power and glory within us. It is that power that attracts a lost and dying world to Christ and praises our Father in heaven.

"My grace is sufficient for you, for my power is made perfect in weakness." 2 Corithians 12:9

32] Fly High and Float Free

Flying in a balloon allows an individual to view God's creation in a way that no other method of flight offers. The experience of gently floating above the earth in the relative quiet and peacefulness of "lighter-than-air" flight approaches angelic proportions. Occurring at significantly lower altitudes and much slower than in a powered aircraft, flying in a balloon affords one a panoramic and extraordinary view of the earth. The view from a balloon is not affected by dirty or scratched windows. Colors are true and crystal clear. Also, during a balloon flight, you can hear the sounds of everyday life far below. While this adds to the uniqueness of the experience, it can also have serious consequences of lulling the pilot into a state of complacency. If the pilot loses concentration, even for a moment, he can lose control of the aircraft.

It is said that a pilot's best friend is altitude. The closer the aircraft stays to the ground, the greater the risk of it becoming entangled in some obstacles. Some pilots have collided with towers, buildings and power lines because they lingered too close to the ground. Although the balloon is very resilient, becoming entangled in any obstacle will usually result in very serious consequences.

Some Christians have become entangled in the obstacles of life with serious and sometimes devastating consequences because they lingered to close to the things that once held them captive to sin. They neglected to "heat" their relationship with God through daily prayer, studying God's Word, and fellowshipping with other believers. These necessary daily activities allow us to rise above the pull of those sinful influences which once held us in captivity, as gravity holds us to the earth. There are potentially serious consequences of lingering too close to those things which once exerted a negative influence on us, placing us in the dangerous position of becoming entangled in them again.

33] Hitting the Target but Missing the Mark

One of the most exciting things you can do with your family is to take them to a balloon rally. Look into the faces of both adults and children alike as they gaze with joy and wonder at the majesty of the "gentle giants" as they fill the sky with color and you will truly appreciate this fact. I have occasionally heard people refer to these events as a "balloon race." As balloons all fly within the same column of air at any given altitude, they all travel at the same speed at any given altitude. Therefore, they cannot race. It's more appropriate to say that balloons "compete" and not race.

By taking advantage of the changes in direction and speed that usually occur as they change altitude, a pilot attempts to maneuver his balloon to a given target. They then attempt to toss a small object called a "baggy" at a target on the ground. The closer you get to the center of the target, the more points you score. After several flights, the person with the most points at the end of the event wins.

A "baggy" is nothing more than a bean bag made of nylon with a long trailing tail. It weighs only 2.7 ounces and is somewhat difficult to throw. Therefore, the closer you fly to a target, the better your chances are of hitting it. Most pilots are very skillful in maneuvering their balloon by altitude and wind directional changes and can easily fly to a target. However, once there, throwing the baggy and hitting the center of that target is another matter.

The baggy is rather light, lacks mass and is not aerodynamic in its design. Therefore, it is easily affected by wind resistance, and if thrown from altitude, it can be significantly affected by wind drift. All of these factors make hitting the mark very difficult.

Pilots employ several techniques of throwing a baggy. Some roll the bean bag into its long nylon tail to increase its mass and lessen wind resistance. They then throw it like a baseball. Other pilots lean over the side of the basket, hold onto the tail of the baggy and twill in a large circular motion with increasing speed to gain momentum. They then let it fly. Regardless of the method, wind resistance, distance to the target, altitude, wind speed, and directional drift all come into play. These factors make this seemingly easy task rather difficult, usually resulting in the pilot "missing the mark" despite his best efforts at maneuvering the balloon to the target.

The Bible has a lot to say about sin and "missing the mark." What is sin? Some religions try and categorize sin according to a particular act. However, the Bible makes two things very clear about sin...

"Knowing what the right thing is to do and then not doing it is sin." James 4:17

"The person who keeps every law of God but makes one little slip, is just as guilty as the person who has broken every law there is." James 2:10

Therefore, no matter the particular details, or the severity of the particular act, sin is sin and worthy of death. The Bible also tells us that all of us are sinners.

"...for all have sinned and fall short of the glory of God." Romans 3:23

The Bible describes sin by the Greek word "hamartia" (ham-ar-tee'-ah). The word comes from the root word "hamartano" (ham-ar-tan'-o); which means, "to miss the mark" (and so as not share in the prize).

So often, we think of sin as intentionally doing something wrong in God's eyes. However, it is clear from the word used to describe it, sin is much more. It can also be failure to "hit the mark" of doing something that is ethically and morally proper, despite our best efforts. Paul, the great apostle who wrote a large part of the New Testament, described his struggle with sin in a very interesting way...

"I am sold into slavery with sin as my owner. I don't understand myself at all, for I really want to do what is right, but I can't. I do what I don't want to, what I hate. I know perfectly well that what I am doing is wrong, and my conscience proves that I agree with these

laws I am breaking. But I can't help myself because I'm no longer doing it. It is sin inside me that is stronger than I am that makes me do these evil things. I know I am rotten through and through so far as my old sinful nature is concerned. No matter which way I turn, I can't make myself do right. I want to but I can't. When I want to do good, I don't; and when I try not to do wrong, I do it anyway. Now, if I am doing what I don't want to, it is plain where the trouble is: sin still has me in its evil grasp. It seems to be a fact of life that when I want to do what is right, I inevitably do what is wrong. I love to do God's will so far as my new nature is concerned; but there is something else deep within me, in my lower nature, that is at war with my mind and wins the fight and makes me a slave to the sin that is still within me. In my mind I want to be God's willing servant, but instead I find myself still enslaved to sin. So you see how it is: my new life tells me to do right, but the old nature that is still inside me loves to sin. Oh, what a terrible predicament I'm in! Who will free me from my slavery to this deadly lower nature? Thank God! It has been done by Jesus Christ our Lord. He has set me free." Romans 7:14-23 [The Living Bible]

It's apparent by Paul's account that "hitting the mark" is very difficult, if not impossible, for us as sinful people to do. Actually, the Bible tells us that only one individual in history has been able to hit the mark and hit it consistently, that was Jesus Christ.

So, if you're pretty good at maneuvering to the target, but are having trouble "hitting the mark" despite your best efforts, maybe you need to employ the great marksman, Jesus Christ, to help you. Let Him who paid the price for our sins "throw the baggy" and "hit the mark" while you sit back and enjoy the ride.

I have come that they may have life, and that they may have it more abundantly. John 10:10

★ (Biblesoft's New Exhaustive Strong's Numbers and Concordance with Expanded GreekHebrew Dictionary. Copyright (c) 1994, Biblesoft and International Bible Translators, Inc.)

34] Can you Hear Me Up There?

One of the most amazing things about flying in a hot air balloon is the quiet and peacefulness of the experience. Unlike an airplane that can be very noisy, except for the occasional blast of the burner, there are no other sounds generated by the aircraft. With the earth acting as a sounding board, and the quietness within the balloon basket, all sounds below seem almost amplified as you gently float high above them. People calling up to you as you quietly float high above them can be clearly heard and understood, and they always seem quite surprised as you answer them from above.

I've often pondered why sounds traveling between two points on the ground do not seem to travel as far or as clearly as sounds passing from the ground into the air. I have never seen a scientific explanation for this phenomenon. I believe that a plausible explanation could be found in the various obstacles on the ground that might absorb, or at least hinder sound transmission, things like trees, bushes and buildings. Sounds passing between the ground and a balloon in flight are not blocked by these objects allowing remarkable distance and clarity to their transmissions.

Once, flying several hundred feet over a golf course, I clearly discerned a conversation between two men far below me. Another time, while doing a city-sponsored flight over the Independence Bowl football game, one team made a touchdown. The roar of the crowd as they cheered the score was deafening. Frequently while flying, I am greeted by multiple greetings of "Hello up there." They are clearly heard, though the various greeters may be several hundred feet below me and several streets apart from each other.

I've wondered if God can hear me when I pray as clearly as I can hear the people on the ground when they call up to me? Also, if it is true that obstacles can hinder communications, are there similar obstacles to my conversations with God? In regards to the statement made by the prophet Isaiah referencing God's ability to "save" and "hear," this might be a question that we all should consider.

"Surely the arm of the LORD is not too short to save, nor his ear too dull to hear. But your iniquities have separated you from your God; and your sins have hidden his face from you, so that he will not hear." Isaiah 59:1-2

35] I Get By With A Little Help From My Friends

Every balloon must have a ground support team, usually consisting of two to five individuals. The team assists the pilot in assembling and launching the aircraft. They follow it through its flight, and then help to disassemble and pack it into the chase vehicle after the balloon lands. They are appropriately called the "chase crew."

Operating a balloon is virtually impossible without a supporting chase crew. Unlike an airplane, flying a balloon is a very social affair and can even be a family endeavor. My first chase crew was composed of my wife, three children, and one other adult. Over time, I had the opportunity to meet others who expressed interest in the sport and eventually became part of our balloon team. Although many had gone onto other endeavors, the relationships forged during the many flights we shared together have resulted in lifelong friendships.

I once had a wall plaque that read: "Friendship doubles our joys and divides our griefs." Nowhere is this more apparent in the sport of ballooning. Chasing a balloon was not always work. My chase crew allowed me to enjoy the blessing of lighter-then-air flight, which I could not have experienced without them. In turn, I shared that blessing with them by occasionally taking each one along for a ride. We indeed had a mutually beneficial relationship.

Ballooning has taught me the value of friends and the benefits of the support friendships offer as we go through the various trials of life. The Bible teaches us these truths. It encourages us to walk through the trials of life together, praying for one another and supporting one another.

"Brethren, if a man be overtaken in a fault, ye which are spiritual, restore such an one in the Spirit of meekness; considering thyself, lest thou also be tempted. Bear ye one another's burdens, and so fulfil the law of Christ." Galatians 6:1-2 [KJV]

"Pray always with all prayer and supplication in the Spirit, and watch there-unto with all perseverance and supplication for all saints." Ephesians 6:18 [KJV]

36] Let Your Light Shine

Although I enjoyed flying my balloon any time I could, I particularly enjoyed the evening flights when people were outside in their yards towards the end of the day. Winds were gentle, and the temperatures were pleasant. Children would run excitedly to get their parents to see the colorful giant slowly floating over their home, waving and calling to us from the ground below. On occasion, I would land in someone's yard [if it was big enough], and their neighbors would come out to witness the excitement of packing up the aircraft. In the days following a flight, it was not unusual for me to receive a letter in the mail with pictures someone took of the balloon as we floated over the city a few days before. As a balloon pilot, you truly were an ambassador of good will to the community.

I have been invited by many social and business-related organizations in my community to speak on the topic of ballooning. While talking to people after my presentation, it was not uncommon for someone to come up to me and relate their experience of seeing my balloon in flight. They would always remember the exact day, location, and specific incident involved in the sighting. It was apparent that the balloon had an effect on whoever witnessed its majesty.

I remember one occasion when an elderly gentleman shared his experience of seeing a balloon at an air show when he was a child. The event occurred many decades ago, yet he clearly remembered the incident and related the description of the sighting as if it happened only a short time ago. I can still remember my first encounter with a hot air balloon. It happened one sunny Sunday afternoon over a corn field in Iowa where I attended graduate school after college. The incident occurred almost fifty years ago. It lasted only a few minutes; yet, I can still see the balloon as it slowly floated a few feet above the cornfield silhouetted against the afternoon sun.

Clearly, balloons have a lasting effect on those who have had an encounter of some sort with them, no matter how casual. Christians should have a similar impact on those we encounter as we drift through life, no matter how casual that encounter may be. In the fifth chapter of the Gospel of Matthew, Jesus commanded: "Let your light so shine before men, that they may see your good works, and glorify your Father which is in heaven." [Matthew 5:16]

Peter, the great Apostle, echoed a similar sentiment in his first Epistle: "But ye are a chosen generation, a royal priesthood, a holy nation, a peculiar people; that ye should shew forth the praises of him who hath called you out of darkness into his marvelous light." [1 Peter 2:9]

A balloon makes a lasting impression on all who witness it. Should we as Christians and ambassadors for Christ not do as much?

37] Off We Go Into the Wild, Blue Yonder

Each time a pilot makes a flight, he looks forward to ever-changing and unknown factors that can influence his flight. As balloon can only fly in one direction, with the wind, before each flight, the pilot must determine the speed and direction of the wind. He must also find out what weather conditions are around the general area of his intended flight to decide if he can safely make the flight.

Each morning we look forward to ever-changing and unknown factors that can influence our lives and the decisions we make throughout our day. Taking a few minutes to plan our day is essential for us as it is for a pilot preparing to make a flight. As Christians, we depend on God's Spirit to carry us through our day just as the wind carries a balloon through its flight. Similar to the weather briefing a pilot receives, the Christian can receive a "spiritual briefing" relative to the possible "operational hindrances" which might be encountered during his daily "flight," and how to deal with them. This information is available to us through God's Word and prayer.

Two biblical passages have inspired me to seek my "spiritual briefing" before I begin my day. The first is Philippians 2:13: "for it is God who works within us both to desire and perform His good will."

The second is Isaiah 30:21: "your ears shall hear a word behind you, saying, this is the way, walk in it, whenever you turn to the right hand or whenever you turn to the left."

These two Biblical statements tell me that God is watching over me and is available to guide and direct me through the problems I might face during my day. Considering the responsibilities and possible devastating consequences a pilot faces every time he flies, I can't imagine that any pilot would attempt to get off the ground without a proper pre-flight planning session. To do so would be irresponsible and insane. Likewise, consider the potential spiritual opposition we face as we go through our day and the spiritual assistance Jesus offers:

"The thief comes to steal, kill, and destroy, but I have come that you may have life and have it more abundantly." [John 10:10]

Why would any Christian not take a few minutes each morning to conduct a proper "pre-day briefing" by spending some time in God's Word and prayer so they can safely plan their day??

The inspirational theme of the U.S. Army Air Corps during WWII is as appropriate today as it was then. "Off we go into the wild, blue yonder." The word "yonder" refers to the "beyond" or "the far side." Each day we face uncertainty and a foe who desires to "steal" our happiness and peace, "kill" us spiritually, and "destroy" or families and lives. [John 10:10] To face these challenges without the assistance of the "abundant life" Jesus Christ offers seems to me to be irresponsible and insane.

38] Rattlesnakes In The Sky

After the conclusion of one of my early training flights in a balloon, I was instructed to make an approach into a field a short distance ahead of us. I allowed the balloon to slowly cool and descended to within several feet above the treetops. I drifted towards the intended landing site, which lay on the other side of a road. As we approached the road, my instructor told me to watch out for the "rattlesnakes in the sky." I curiously replied, "What?" He reiterated, "The rattlesnakes in the sky, ….power-lines! If you get to close to them, they'll bite you."

Power-lines are the number one obstacle that causes concern to a balloon pilot. While balloons very seldom come in contact with them, when they do, the power-lines usually win and with potentially disastrous results… much like rattlesnakes and people. Power-lines can easily be hidden by trees, and we were flying very close to the tops of the trees that surrounded the field we intended to land in. We were also flying towards a road. Power-lines usually can be found along a road. The almost certain possibility that they lay hidden up ahead presented a potential threat and warranted my instructor's concern.

As we approached the road we had to cross over to get into the intended landing field, I began to look for the power-lines. As suspected, there they were! I kept the balloon under control, passed over them at a safe distance, then descended into the field for a gentle and safe landing.

Knowing where power-line usually can be found is a balloon pilot's advantage. However, looking out for them is another matter. What good is it to know that rattlesnakes usually reside near a rock or under a fallen tree trunk if you ignore that information and clumsily blunder into their territory? A well-respected friend once told me,

"Knowledge without application is useless information!"

Although power-lines are a significant concern to a balloon pilot, they are not the only concern. Actually, any obstacle on the ground presents a potential threat to a balloon, and needs to be avoided by keeping a safe distance from them. Therefore, a balloon pilot is taught that "altitude is your friend." The best way to avoid a problem…. is to avoid the problem! If you know it's there, stay away from it.

How often Christians are "bitten" by an old problem [lust, anger, pride, greed] by lingering to close to the source of that problem. The Bible tells us that Christ has saved us from sin, and those sinful practices no longer have power over us, ...unless we allow them to.

But now you are free from the power of sin and are slaves of God, and his benefits to you include holiness and everlasting life. Romans 6:22

39] The Early Bird Catches The Worm

The greatest danger to balloon flight is high winds. A balloon flies within a column of air. It doesn't move through the air like an airplane, it moves with the air. The faster the air is moving, the faster the balloon moves also. The faster a balloon moves when it touches down, the greater the chance of damage to the aircraft and the passengers in it.

One method a balloon pilot uses to slow the balloon's forward motion before landing is to drag the basket below the balloon through the tops of the trees. Aside from that method, the friction between the balloon and ground is the only other means of slowing the forward motion of the aircraft. The faster the balloon moves when it touches down, the longer it will take to slow and eventually stop the aircraft. The longer the balloon drags along the ground before it stops, the greater the danger of it coming in contact with something on the ground, which will damage that object, the balloon, or both.

If you are fortunate enough to fly in an open area like New Mexico where you have large landing areas with little or no obstructions, then flights in higher winds are possible. However, in other areas where landing sites are limited to vacant fields of an acre [or less], sporting fields or parking lots, care must be taken to fly in gentle winds of eight miles an hour or less.

Balloonists regularly study the weather and look for periods of relatively calm winds to fly in. Generally, winds are at their calmest in the morning from sunrise to about two hours after sunrise, and in the evening from about two hours before sunset to sunset. However, you are more likely to see a balloon in the early morning when the air is cool, and wind speeds are low.

When I was thirty years old, I came to understand who Jesus Christ was and what he had done for me by dying on a cross to pay the price for my sins. I began a quest to learn all I could about my creator and savior and the relationship I could have with Him. I joined a church and met a man who I had a short friendship with before he went away to seminary. His name was Randy Driggers. He was my first mentor in the Christian faith. During the early days of our friendship, Randy asked me a question that changed my life. He asked if I had a "quiet time" in the morning. I had no idea what he was talking about and expressed my ignorance of that fact.

Randy explained to me that it was a time in the early morning when things tend to be quiet, and we can spend quality time with God in study, prayer, and meditation. He told me that it was the time to prepare for the day ahead and seek God's guidance for the trials and various temptations we might face throughout that day. I immediately began a quiet time and have continued it now for nearly forty five years. It has been unquestionably the most essential element in my Christian development. [Thank You Randy where ever you are].

The concept of a quiet time is not foreign to the Bible. Jesus rose early to converse with His Father. Also, David, Israel's greatest king wrote about his early morning quiet times.

"In the morning, O LORD, you hear my voice; in the morning I lay my requests before you and wait in expectation." Psalms 5:3

While it is true that God is with us always, it is also true that so are the many troubling issues and distractions that surround us throughout our day. I find that God's "still, small voice" is best heard early before those issues and distractions begin. Also, my friend Randy once told me that the best time to prepare for a battle is before it begins. Another reason for early quiet time is to prepare for the onset of the "spiritual warfare" we all face daily. [Ephesians 6:10-18]

Early in my ballooning career, I learned to love my early morning flights when the earth is still, the air is cool and clear, and the winds are gentle and true. I've also learned to love my early morning quiet times when my mind is rested and calm, the day ahead is full of promise, ...and there are no distractions [as everyone else is still asleep]

40] The Hare & Hound

In 1992 I had the privilege of being the rookie pilot in the Great Texas Balloon Race. This event is held in Longview, Texas, each July. It is considered to be one of the most distinguished hot air balloon related events in the country. The event is a "closed" event with "invitation only" acceptance. It usually attracts 75 pilots, nearly half being past U.S. National and World Champions. The Great Texas Balloon Race is hosted by Dr. Bill Bussey, a holder of fifteen world records and arguably one of the finest, if not the finest hot air balloon pilots in the world.

On the first day of the competition, Dr. Bussey called a "Hare & Hound" task. The purpose of the task was for him to launch approximately fifteen minutes before the rest of the field. After flying for a short distance, he was to land, place a large target out in a field, then take off again to maneuver to a second target of his choice.

Sitting on the ground with the rest of the 74 pilots in attendance, I watched as Dr. Bussey inflated, then launched his balloon. I carefully observed his altitude and direction as he slowly drifted away. If I was to "score," I would have to duplicate his flight path. My balloon was assembled and ready to be inflated. After fifteen minutes, inflation fans began to roar, and colorful mounds of fabric began to dot the field. Soon the balloons were inflated, and the sound of the burners announced the impending launch.

One by one, the balloons climbed into the air. I happened to be in the middle of the pack.

Looking out from about five hundred feet, I could clearly make out where Dr. Bussey had landed and had placed the first target. His balloon then climbed back into the sky to maneuver to another field where the second target would be placed. Visually marking the area where his balloon had been a minute before, I [along with every other pilot] proceeded to maneuver our balloons to that spot. One by one, the balloons descended, made their run on the target, threw their "baggies," and then climbed back up to altitude to fly to the second target.

Being the rookie pilot that year, I was quite pleased as my baggie landed only a foot and a half from the center of the target. As I climbed out again, I focused my attention on the balloons ahead of me to reach their altitude. I assumed that they were aware of the second target, and I wanted to be sure to fly in the same direction of drift they were in. Once at altitude, I looked out ahead to find Dr. Bussey's balloon to determine where the second target was [or would be placed], however, I could not find it. After several minutes of searching the horizon without any luck, I called to a friend of mine flying off to my right, "Can you see him?" "No," was the reply! Soon a transmission came across the radio from another pilot, "Does anyone see him?" Again the answer was a short "No!" Then someone radioed, "There he is!" Another voice over the radio inquired, "Where?" The shocking reply was, "He's at our eight O-clock." I looked towards that position. There was Dr. Bussey's balloon about a half-mile to the left of all of us, and behind us! Another pilot called out in a surprised voice: "How in the world did he get there?" ...how indeed?

Apparently, the winds above us were blowing at a tangent to the easterly direction we were all heading in. After placing the first target out, Dr. Bussey climbed to about two thousand feet and caught the invisible southwesterly river of wind that was well above us. None of us caught his maneuver as we were all focused on where he had been and not where he was going next. The moral of the story was, no one was able to maneuver their balloons in time to duplicate Dr. Bussey's maneuver, and we all missed the second target. What did I learn from this experience? Always keep focused on the lead balloon, not on where it had been, and not on the balloons around you.

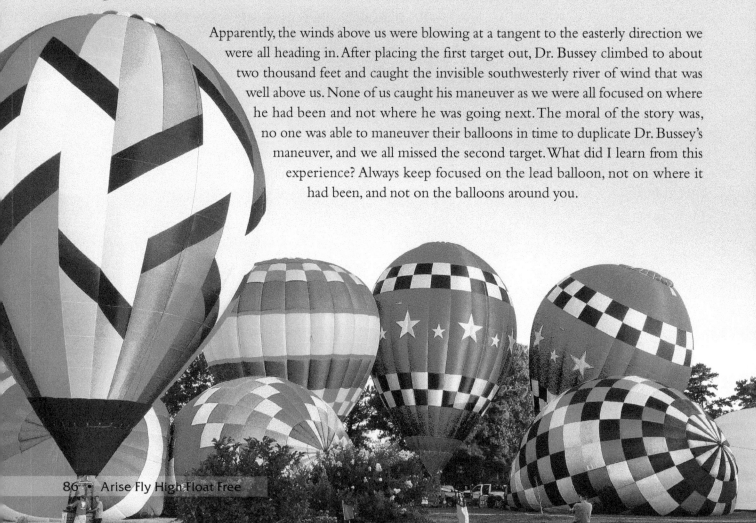

So often in Christianity, we take our lead from those around us and get caught up in "church." I've noticed that people in different churches tend to pray the same way, using the same phrases and emphasizing the same priorities. We lose our individuality and begin to follow the leadership of men instead of the leadership of Christ.

The lesson here should be obvious. We need to keep our eye on Christ and not on those around us. God has a plan for each of us personally. He has also given each of us the commission to be "ministers of reconciliation to a lost and dying world." [2 Corinthians 5:17-18].

We do this by living daily in a way that lets "our light so shine before men so they might see our good works and glorify our Father in heaven." [Matthew 5:16]. The way we conduct ourselves every day should raise a curiosity in others as to why we are the way we are. Our actions and attitudes should cause them to "ask for the reason of the hope that is in us." [1 Peter 3:15] We should always be prepared to give them that reason in a gentle and respectful manner.

Remember: If you keep your eye on the lead balloon and you will always know where the targets are so you can score.

It is with much appreciation that I would like to acknowledge Dr. Bill Bussey, my friend and mentor in Hot Air Ballooning. Without Dr. Bussey this publication would not be possible. He is arguably one of the most outstanding balloonists in the entire world. He currently holds fifteen world and thirty U.S. National records for his achievements in Hot Air Ballooning. He is a distinguished member of the Texas Aviation, and the United States Hot Air Balloon Hall of Fame.

Dr. Bussey is the founder of the Great Texas Balloon race which is held in Longview, Texas, each July. The Great Texas Balloon Race is one of the most respected Hot Air Balloon events in the world. All participants are accepted on their past achievements in the sport, with a large percentage being past U.S. and/or World Hot Air Balloon Champions. Doctor Bussey is also the founder of the renowned "Balloon Glow," which is seen in virtually every Hot Air Balloon event in the world. He is a recipient of the 40 year "Ed Yost Master Pilot's Award" issued by the Balloon Federation of America, and a two-time recipient of the "Shields-Trauger Memorial Award." He has received the prestigious "Montgolfier Diploma," which is the highest honor awarded to a Hot Air Balloonist.

In addition to flying balloons, Dr. Bussey is also an instrument and multi-engine rated airplane pilot and has received the 50 years Wright Brothers Master Pilot's Award issued by the United States Federal Aviation Administration.

41] The Terminal Descent

One of the techniques a student pilot must master when learning to fly a balloon is recovering from a terminal descent. What is a terminal descent? It is the rate of descent a balloon will attain in "feet-per-minute" when the balloon is allowed to cool to the point of its inability to sustain lift. Depending on the balloon's size and shape, that rate can vary from several hundred to more than a thousand feet per minute. Most balloons only fly at an altitude of a thousand feet or less, and obstacles on the ground can tower to a height of a hundred feet or more. An inattentive pilot, who allows the balloon to cool beyond its capacity to sustain life, can find himself falling at such a rate of speed that he only has seconds to correct and recover from the descent before crashing into some obstacle below.

Unlike an airplane which glides to a lower altitude at a constant rate of descent, while a balloon will fall at an exponential rate till the resistance of the air against its side equals its mass. The balloon will then stabilize at a constant rate of descent, much like a parachute.

When training a student pilot to recover from a terminal descent, the instructor usually takes the balloon to several thousand feet. The balloon is allowed to cool till a terminal descent is established. As the descent rapidly increases, the instructor and student carefully observe the vertical speed indicator [one of the flight instruments in the balloon basket]. When the rate of descent stabilizes, the balloon is in terminal descent. The instructor then tells the student to recover from the descent at a particular altitude, ...say a thousand feet. The balloon will take several seconds of a constant blast of the burner to heat the air sufficiently to regain life. Therefore, the burn will have to be initiated several hundred feet above the target altitude of recovery. The intent is to determine how soon a burn must be initiated before reaching the target altitude of recovery. This allows a student to better learn the operational characteristic of the aircraft.

There are several essential lessons to be learned by this exercise. One is to obviously learn to recover from a terminal descent. Another is to learn to recognize its beginnings so it can be avoided and/or to initiate recovery procedures as soon as possible to minimize altitude loss. Another important lesson is to demonstrate how rapidly a terminal descent can sneak up on you and demonstrate how fast a balloon can fall out of the sky and into some obstacle below. Finally, the exercise is invaluable in teaching the student how difficult it can be to regain lift once lost. This stresses the need for constant vigilance by the pilot to avoid this situation in the first place.

Terminal descents are not restricted to balloons; they are also very common in Christianity. However, they are not referred to as a terminal descent, but as being "backslidden." They occur when a person loses their fervor for Christ and regresses back into the life style and carnal practices from which they were saved. Like a balloon, a terminal descent in Christianity begins very subtly but progresses rapidly into a full-fledged fall. Therefore, it is very important for Christians to always be vigilant and keep a consistent input from the source of their power, God's Word. This assures that they will stay "HOT" and maintain a consistent walk with Christ.

42] "Do or do not, ...there is no try!"

In one of the Star Wars movies, the great Jedi master "Yoda" is reluctantly training a young disciple, Luke Skywalker. Luke attempts to lift his Star Fighter out of a bog with just his mind's power. Yoda encourages him when his attempt fails, and Luke answers with "I will try." Yoda's response lends itself well to flying a hot air balloon, "Do or do not...there is no try!"

As a pilot prepares to land, he can release heat from the balloon to control its rate of descent into a landing site. If one carefully examines a balloon, they will notice that there is a large opening at the top of the balloon. This is to allow air to easily pass through the balloon. During the flight, this opening is "sealed" by a parachute-like structure. It is attached along the perimeter, and several inches below the opening. It is slightly larger in circumference than the opening so that when the heated air from the burner rises, it pushes against it, causing it to seal the opening. When sealed, it holds the heated air inside the balloon. As the heated air is less dense than the cooler air surrounding it, it raises. As it does, it lifts the balloon and all of its contents with it.

A rope is attached to the "parachute-like" structure, referred to as "the vent line." It hangs in the basket and is usually red for a reason. When a faster-than-normal descent is required, the pilot can pull on the rope, breaking the seal above him. This action allows the heated air to escape. This reduces lift, allowing the balloon to descend at an accelerated rate. The speed of descent is proportionate to the amount of heated air that is released.

As a balloon slowly drifts through the sky, there is no way to slow its forward progress. It persistently forges ahead with the wind at its back. Once a flight nears completion, a pilot must select a landing site. The selection process can involve several crucial factors that must be quickly considered. Once the balloon passes a potential landing site, three is no way to turn it around for a second attempt.

When a potential landing site is selected, the pilot must make a controlled approach into the site. He takes in consideration the direction of the drift of the balloon towards the site, ...the speed of the balloon as it enters the lower altitude, ...the altitude he must safely maintain over any structures in his flight path, ...and any possible interference from obstructions such as trees, bushes, buildings, etc. at the intended landing site.

The pilot must also consider the size of the area he intends to land in. Once on the ground, the balloon's forward momentum can cause it to "drag" for a distance before it comes to a stop. How far the balloon might drag is directly dependent on wind speed. A balloon has no brakes, and once the balloon ceases to fly, it can become a sail.

When the balloon stops and begins to cool, it is laid down in front of the basket. Therefore the pilot must stop the balloon's forward momentum within a distance equal to or greater than its height. He does this by pulling on the vent line to allow the heated air to escape. This is called "venting." as the aircraft drags across the ground. The faster the air is released, the shorter the balloon's distance will drag before coming to a stop. A rapid stop will prevent the balloon from coming in contact with any object that might lie in its path. If the pilot does not stop the balloon in time, the balloon's weight and the force it can potentially exert against some object in its path will most definitely cause an alteration to the structure of the object, the balloon, ...or both!

When all of the factors associated with landing the balloon are taken into consideration and the pilot determines that it is safe to land the balloon, he must commit to the landing site. Once the heat is vented, the balloon can no longer sustain lift and will descend. Replacing enough heat in the balloon to regain lift takes time. As the balloon is at such a low altitude during the landing sequence, that crucial amount of time is not available. Therefore, once the final descent begins, it is impossible to stop. The balloon is coming down and will land [therefore, there is no "try"]. Many student pilots miss a good landing site because they hesitated to decide to commit to a site and go drifting by it. Like Yoda, my response to a missed landing is usually somewhat unsympathetic. I remind them that failure to make a decision is a decision in itself; ....it is a decision to do nothing.

In the region where I fly, a missed landing site can be a potentially serious error. It is surrounded by large wooded areas, ...having few open fields [and most filled with livestock], ...three large lakes, ...a meandering river, ...three major airports [one being an Air Force Base with restricted access], ...a large metropolitan area with very high buildings, ...and some very large Louisiana swampy areas that are filled with "things" that will eat you and your balloon. A student pilot must learn to make quick decisions [or sell their balloon and buy a boat]. After-all, you never know when the next acceptable landing site might come along, [...or not!] So, if one presents itself, you had better take advantage of it. More than one pilot in this area has landed in a place that required several hours and many volunteers to retrieve his aircraft. All it takes to convince a student of the seriousness of making a quick decision is to land their expensive balloon in a swamp one time.

"Failure to make a decision is a decision in itself,
...it is a decision to do nothing."

It can be argued that a decision to do nothing is the rejection of an opportunity. Either you take advantage of it, or you miss the opportunity. There is no second chance at a potential landing site. Possibly another will come along, ...but possibly not. It is much better to attempt a landing while the balloon is under your control. Once you are out of fuel, your opportunities are over. Either you take advantage of your landing opportunities now, or a landing site will be chosen for you when your fuel runs out.

In reality, we all face many decisions every day. Some have serious consequences, some do not. One decision that has very serious consequences and we all must individually face is what we do with this Jesus Christ? God offers us the opportunity to learn who Jesus is, what he did, and why he did it.

"For God so loved the world that he gave his one and only Son, that whoever believes in him shall not perish but have eternal life. For God did not send his Son into the world to condemn the world, but to save the world through him." John 3:16-17

The Bible also tells us about an opportunity that is available to us because of what Jesus did.

"I tell you the truth, whoever hears my words and believes in him who sent me has eternal life and will not be condemned; he has crossed over from death to life." John 5:24-25

"If you confess with your mouth, "Jesus is Lord," and believe in your heart that God raised him from the dead, you will be saved. For it is with your heart that you believe and are justified,

and it is with your mouth that you confess and are saved. As the Scripture says, "Anyone who trusts in him will never be put to shame." For there is no difference between Jew and Gentile
the same Lord is Lord of all and richly blesses all who call on him, for, "who-so-ever calls on the name of the Lord will be saved." Romans 10:9-13

Therefore, we are all faced with the decision regarding Jesus Christ. As you ponder this decision, remember that no decision is a decision to do nothing, and a decision to do nothing is a rejection of an opportunity. Consider that fact in regards to what Jesus Himself said in the Gospel of Luke…."He who is not with me is against me," Luke 11:23
So, I will conclude with this thought: In the words of the great Jedi master Yoda, …..

"Do or do not, there may be no…I'll think about it later." [A little poetic license here in paraphrase]

Unlike a balloon, in life we do not get a "second chance" at where we will ultimately conclude our life's flight. We can either choose where we will spend eternity now and commit to it, or that choice will be made for us when our "fuel" runs out.

43] Along For The Ride

It was a beautiful morning with the sun just below the horizon, sending out its golden rays across a clear blue sky. The morning's flight plan was to do an instructional flight with a student who was preparing to take his final "check ride" before getting his private pilot's license. We sent up a small balloon called a "Pibal" [which is short for " Pilot Balloon] to determine the direction and speed of the wind. As the small helium-filled balloon slowly drifted upwards, it revealed a southwesterly drift close to the ground of about two miles an hour. As it climbed higher, its direction changed to northwesterly with an increase in speed of about seven miles an hour….a perfect scenario for lighter-than-air flight.

We chose a launch site that would take us over some open fields that would allow the student to drift close to the ground, practicing what is referred to as "contour flying." It is a difficult exercise that requires intense concentration as so to maintain an altitude very close to the ground without letting the balloon cool and make contact with the ground. After flying over those fields, we intended to climb to a higher altitude, turn to the northwest, fly for a while in the higher winds, then descend back into the slower winds and look for a field to land in.

We drove out to the launch site we had selected. We assembled and inflated the balloon, then launched into the gentle breeze which proved to be true to our observations with the small Pibal we had earlier sent up. The first part of our flight went as planned. However, as we climbed to a higher altitude to complete the second part of our flight plan, something very surprising and entirely unexpected occurred. Instead of the balloon gently turning to the northwest, it shuddered as if it was hit from the side by a truck. It then turned to the west and picked up speed. We had entered a wind shear, an invisible river of air traveling in a different direction and at a very high speed.

After the initial shock of the directional and speed change, the balloon settled down to a calm drift as it was now totally engulfed by the new layer of wind it had entered. As the ground sped by below, we quietly floated along with no perceivable movement, enjoying the ride. Forty minutes later, we descended out of that wind shear and into a much slower breeze. We eventually landed in the back yard of a house in East Texas some fifty miles away from where we launched. The balloon had traveled over ten times the distance initially intended, allowing us to enjoy the most unexpected and memorable flight.

The direction and speed of a balloon flight is determined by layer of wind it flies in. The Spirit of God within a man or woman determines the "direction and speed" of their life. The Bible tells us:

"...for it is God who works in you both to will and to act according to his good purpose." [Philippians 2:13]

Sometimes God's direction may not be according to our plans and may come as a shock. However, once we are "inside" God's will, things tend to calm down. We can settle back and "enjoy the ride." It is amazing what we might unexpectedly experience when we "go with the flow" and allow God to work His will in us.

"For I know the plans I have for you," declares the LORD, " plans to prosper you and not to harm you, plans to give you hope and a future. Then you will call upon me and come and pray to me, and I will listen to you. You will seek me and find me when you seek me with all your heart." Jeremiah 29:11-13

44] A Safe Landing....The Perfect Ending to a Perfect Flight

Team Work:

All balloon flights are assisted by a ground support crew. As the balloon flies with the wind and not against it, a ground crew in a "chase vehicle" is necessary. They follow the pilot through his flight. They provide the pilot with valuable information regarding ground conditions during the flight, and assist him with the landing and "pack-up" of the aircraft after a flight is concluded.

The chase crew also provides the pilot with necessary information regarding the condition of an intended landing site. From a thousand feet, a field might take on the appearance of a manicured golf course, but may actually contain weeds several feet high. It also may be covered with several inches of water or mud making extraction of the aircraft difficult or impossible. The intended landing area might be surrounded by a fence with a locked gate. It may contain livestock [like the territorial bull I once encountered during one of my early flights....but that's another story]. The potential landing field may be surrounded by high trees which can conceal power lines on the approach into the field. Or, there may be a single power line running across the field that is so narrow it is difficult to see. It should be apparent that the pilot and crew work together as a team to ensure a safe and enjoyable flight.

Communication:

Chasing a balloon can be challenging. Aside from the changes in direction that usually accompanies changes in altitude, a balloon otherwise flies in a straight line as it crosses fields, lakes, rivers, cities, and towns. To keep up with the balloon, a chase vehicle may have to drive around these obstacles, or follow roads that twist and turn. Sometimes a balloon will fly over densely forested areas where there are no roads. Populated areas present other problems such as traffic, railroad crossings, stop lights, and areas of construction. Although the chase crew can travel faster, all of these obstructions make it difficult for the chase crew to keep up with the balloon it is supporting.

Other factors that make chasing a balloon challenging are tall trees and buildings which block the crews "line-of-sight." Therefore, it is not always possible for the crew to keep in visual contact with the aircraft. At times they must assume it is continuing in the direction it had been flying in. However, if the pilot changes altitude for any reason, the balloons direction can change as well.

Even when the balloon is clearly seen, it can be difficult to determine the direction it is flying in. While it may appear to be going in one direction, it may actually be going in a direction very different from the one perceived. If the chase crew is detained for any reason and cannot keep up with the balloon, it can quickly lose visual contact with the aircraft altogether. This is especially true as the balloon descends into a landing site.

All of these factors require that the chase crew keep in constant contact with the pilot by radio, which allows the pilot to alert the crew to potential directional changes to his flight path, or warn them of any obstructions along their chase route. There were times that I instructed my chase crew to do something that made no sense to them from their point of view. One example was making a turn at an intersection that seemed to take them in a direction different from the one I was heading in. What they could not see was some road obstruction up ahead of them that would have placed them in traffic, preventing them from being at the landing site when I needed them. Although the directional change made no sense to them, it was perfectly obvious to me from my vantage point high above all the visual obstacles which surrounded them.

Conclusion:

As we go through life, we cannot see what lies ahead one day, one hour or even one minute. Things can occur so quickly that we may not be aware of what just happened until it is too late. How often I have wished that I could press "delete" or "backspace" and start over. God knows life can be tough. Sometimes difficult and challenging situations must be dealt with. Here are three verses which demonstrates that God cares about us and what we face daily:

"No temptation has seized you except what is common to man. And God is faithful; he will not let you be tempted beyond what you can bear. But when you are tempted, he will also provide a way out so that you can stand up under it." 1 Corinthians 10:13

"Because he [Christ] himself suffered when he was tempted, he is able to help those who are being tempted." Hebrews 2:17-18

"Come to me, all you who are weary and burdened, and I will give you rest. Take my yoke upon you and learn from me, for I am gentle and humble in heart, and you will find rest for your souls. For my yoke is easy and my burden is light." Matthew 11:28-29

God has the advantage of looking down on our lives and seeing them from a different perspective. God can see things we cannot. His "still small voice" within us can warn us of potential problems, direct us through a crisis and give us the wisdom to go through life victoriously. To benefit from His guidance, we must be in constant communication with God through prayer, always listening for His "still, small voice." We must also be willing to be obedient and follow His direction.

"Your word is a lamp to my feet and a light for my path." Psalms 119:105

Have you ever experienced a day when everything seemed to be going wrong? ...when nothing you planned seemed to be turning out right, and there seemed to be some unseen force inhibiting your plans, something that almost seemed to be working against you? If you are like me, you probably reacted with irritation and possibly even some degree of anger. My ballooning experiences have taught me that just because my plans might not be going the way I intended, they might not be going wrong. I have learned to stop and consider God's promises to guide, direct, and protect me as I move through my day. When things change or seem to be going wrong, I "turn on my spiritual radio," [prayer] and listen for God's "still small voice" which can quietly direct my spirit to a "safe landing site."

After a balloon flight, my crew and I would go out for something to eat and review our flight. We would talk about what went wrong and what went right. What did we learn from the flight that would make us better at what we do? I have tried to continue that practice in my day-to-day life. As I conclude my day, I sit quietly with a cup of coffee, thinking about my day. What went right, what went wrong, and what did I learn from my "flight" that day?

It has been said that hindsight has "20-20 vision." Unfortunately, we cannot go backward and live our lives over to correct mistakes. However, we can learn from our mistakes so we don't repeat them. Hindsight can teach us to look for potential problems and avoid them. It also teaches us how to deal with them when they do occur.

When I was going through "ground school" for my airplane pilots license over fifty years ago, I was told that 98% of any flight occurred before the pilot ever left the ground. The purpose of a "pre-flight planning session," was to consider any problems that could occur during the flight and how to deal with them if they did occur. That training has served me well throughout my life, not only with my flying but also with life itself.

Spending time in God's Word before my day begins has helped me to prepare for the day ahead. It provides wisdom to not only avoid, but also deal with issues that seem to arise unexpectedly throughout the day. I have found that God's Word is more than a history book. It is an instruction book on how to live a successful and prosperous life. It helps me to make right decisions based on Biblical principles. It gives me the assurance to know that God is directing and protecting me.

The years I spent flying hot air balloons have shown me that life is a lot like flying. Weather briefings and pre-flight planning has allowed me to safely fly both airplanes and balloons for half a century without one accident or even minor injury. Life, like the weather, has a nasty habit of changing rapidly and unexpectedly. When it does, it pays to have a "back-up plan." Take the time to do a "pre-flight" planning session [a quiet time] before your day begins, and a "post-flight evaluation" [an evening quiet time] after your day concludes so that you can...

Arise

.... out of the sinful influences, desires and emotional passions the world shackles us with,

Fly high

... above the cares and troubles our enemy Satan would try us with, and....

Float FREE

...through this life, resting peacefully in God's loving grace.

Author Bio:

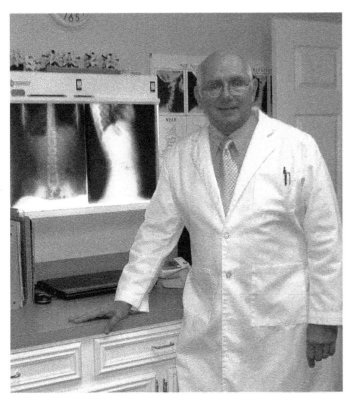

Over the past forty four years, Dr. Wojcik has spoken in churches, Bible, and Pastor Conferences on the similarities of the human body and the church. He hosted a weekly radio program titled "The Living Body of Christ," utilizing physicians of various specialties to explore the similarities between the human body and the church. He has presented a program on the "Anatomical and Physiological Aspects of Crucifixion" in over two hundred churches. He now turns his attention to the similarities between "lighter-than-air" flight and the Christian experience. His unique ability to see God's presence in everyday life brings an interesting twist to this educational, inspirational, and entertaining book.

Utilizing fifty colorful photographs which he has taken over the years, his book introduces the reader to all the intricacies of flying a hot air balloon. He explains how a balloon overcomes the law of gravity by being filled with super-heated air, and maneuvers freely through the sky utilizing only the wind to direct it. He then explores the similarities of how an individual can overcome the law of sin by being filled with God's Holy Spirit, and maneuver successfully through life by the directing power of God.

Dr. Wojcik is a commercially rated airplane and hot air balloon pilot with 54 years of aviation experience. He has flown in various types of aircraft ranging from civil aviation, antique World War II vintage, and modern day jet aircraft. He is a recipient of the "Wright Brothers Master Pilot Award" which is issued by the United State Federal Aviation Administration. This prestigious award is the highest honor issued to pilots who, for fifty years, have demonstrated "professionalism, skill and expertise in piloting an aircraft."

Lightning Source UK Ltd.
Milton Keynes UK
UKHW020708290121
377891UK00005B/50